THE MARKET-DRIVEN CHURCH

the

MARKET-
DRIVEN
CHURCH

The Worldly Influence of Modern Culture
on the Church in America

UDO W. MIDDELMANN

CROSSWAY BOOKS

A DIVISION OF
GOOD NEWS PUBLISHERS
WHEATON, ILLINOIS

Library of Congress Cataloging-in-Publication Data
Middelmann, Udo W., 1940-
    The market-driven church : the worldly influence of modern culture on the church in America / Udo W. Middelmann.
      p. cm.
    ISBN 1-58134-509-7
    1.Christianity and culture—United States. 2. Church—Biblical teaching. I. Title.
BR517.M53   2004
277.3'083—dc22
                        2003022180

BP		13	12	11	10	09	08	07	06	05	04
15	14	13	12	11	10	9	8	7	6	5	4	3	2	1

To my children
Natasha, Samantha, Naomi, Hannah, and Isaac

Like many previous generations,
"you received the word of God, which you heard from us . . .
not as the word of men but as what it really is,
the word of God"
(1 THESSALONIANS 2:13)

CONTENTS

1

ATTRACTION AND
REPULSION

No other country in the Western world is so openly religious as
America. The country has a history of immigrants who sought
the free exercise of religion as much as freedom from religious and ideological persecution elsewhere. Even those who looked primarily for
more liberal and economic opportunities often left behind a cultural
context of tight rules and traditional patterns, which were founded on
particular religious worldviews. America's institutions and history, her
mission before the world, and her enthusiasm to engage and confront
evil around the globe play out before a background of profound specific religious convictions about human life, the rights of individuals,
and the rule of law. These were brought into the human consciousness
largely through the teaching of the Bible as the fitting explanation of
man's origin and destiny.

The Bible's account was and is not limited to personal situations
and private faith. The multitude of religious bodies, the differences
between denominations, the constitutionally guaranteed freedom of,
not from, religion has so far not diminished the memory of a biblical view of all aspects of life in American history and much of the
present public life. There is one church for every 850 to 900 citizens
in the country,[1] roughly the same ratio as medical doctors to people
in Switzerland. Churches reach the mind and calm the soul in the

same ratio as doctors deal with physical problems. We are all well provided for.

References to concepts and realities that only the Bible talks about and has introduced to human life are found in conversations, in speeches, in the lives of citizens. Personal rights, the rule of law to serve justice, a purpose to be expressed through changing individual efforts, and a reality of new beginnings are rooted in a biblical view of man in history. Not counting the use of God's name, etc. in profanity, the whole country expresses some type of religious faith, from "God bless America" to huge crowded parking lots around churches on Sundays. A smaller number still come together several times on other days of the week. Uncounted gatherings continue this religious interest and occupation before the public's eye in the informal settings of private homes for Bible studies, prayer groups, and discussion.

A steady stream of people has come from all over the world in pursuit of freer possibilities than those available in their own countries, including the practice of their Christian or non-Christian or Jewish religious views. These views and experiences are freely entered into public discourse and election campaigns. Present holders of public office and hopeful candidates for future government positions often include their religious convictions in their resumé. They contribute to the market of ideas even outside the church. They are nurtured by a whole industry of Christian book and music publishers, camps and retreats, seminars, conferences, and private parochial schools. What is believed is brought to bear on public life even without an official religious orientation. This affects industry, government, and education. What people believe about the basic building blocks of life has consequences in choices, attitudes, and debates for better and for worse.

Europe has shown her marvelous cathedrals and architectural details in church buildings through the centuries since Christianity spread across the continent. Education touches on Christianity as part of public school curricula, though what is more specifically "Christian" has more often recently been replaced by "religious" histories to include Islam, Buddhism, and other tribal religions. Christian teaching has changed the way people look at life, work, and social realities. Athens and Rome laid many foundations, but Jerusalem gave rise to a practical life of work and art, of lawful rule and the rights of individuals. The teaching of Judaism and Christianity introduced the concept of a purposeful linear history, of moral judgment, and of a hope in life that dismantled the dominant, fatalistic outlook of Greece, Rome, and Germanic paganism. Under Christian teaching the emphasis became life instead of death, law instead of power, and intelligence instead of intellectualism.

At the same time *beginnings*, *invention*, and *discovery* became central perspectives that replaced habit, repetition, and fate. The church gave encouragement, space, and funds to develop an economic, social, and artistic view of this priority of man. It furthered markets and skills, education and a social conscience. Around the teaching of Christianity was continued the emphasis of Jewish thought about the central value of life and resistance against death. The "in the beginning" words of Genesis and of St. John's Gospel gave birth to a purposeful and linear view of history toward judgment and redemption. Churches and monasteries influenced the land and its people with a unique focus on life. This was pursued through the copying and editing of old manuscripts for the preservation of knowledge. Health concerns for the public drove the search for hygiene through medicinal potions for the stomach such as Cointreau, Chartreuse, and Benedictine. We now know these only as liqueurs.

Europe also had a strong Christian base that was founded on the teaching of the Bible and applied through the choices of persons in the midst of the ups and downs of history. There was never a smooth progress or a distinguishable line of advance of Christianity over paganism. Yet the power of ideas worked a change of heart and mind first. Then hands that held the plow, the chisel, and the sword brought food to the poor and pointed out the biblical view of things in the arts and trades. The mind and the hands laid the foundation for a culture that became specifically different from others. At its core was a different view of man, life and death, the mind and rationality, law and rule, and history.

Witnesses of Christianity surround the traveler in Europe in every public space. The churches, the old roads, the enclosed towns and older hospitals, even the museums are brought forth from a Christian view of life. But so are rules of politeness, self-discipline, pride in workmanship, and a healthy bit of humility, apart from occasional and tragic temptations to impose a "perfect solution" for society. Even when personal convictions of Christianity diminish or fail as a result of liberal theology and moral uncertainties, the European will still have the silent, powerful witness of history, which serves, with its Christian content, both as a restraint and an encouraging reminder.

The new world depends for restraints and reminders much more on the personal belief and acts of the religious person, whether Christian or believing Jew. Vibrancy and freshness, personal engagement and activities create a fabric of life. But there is a danger that without outside and historic restraints such religious interest is only personal, and therefore private, subject much more to the changing directions of the winds of culture than to a sense of continuity of truth from the beginning. Church and theology, personal faith and its expressions, ministries and their purposes are much more likely to be affected, even diluted, by what a society embraces as current values and imagined futures. When the whole society looks ahead for what it wishes to achieve, it tends to forget the limitations of reality and to pursue imagination, wishful thinking, and utopia.

The Bible starts at the beginning. There the stage is set for us as actors. Our characters are established in the stage notes of the book of Genesis. Man is both glorious and the crown of creation, but he is now also the child of Adam and Eve, broken and in need of moral and physical transformation. We are not free to start with ourselves and then assume that our best ideals should be embraced or can be realized. The Bible talks about the need for good ideas about life but never presents the possibility of achieving the ideal through human action. Failure to recognize this has brought about the tragic and inhuman idealisms pursued by "new people in a new world" and also by Marxist-Leninism, Fascism, and the idea that the will of the people leads to moral government.

Alexis de Tocqueville (1805-1859) came to America and looked around for a brief nine months. He shared his views and findings in his book *Democracy in America* (two volumes). What he observed, analyzed, and wrote about was intended for a European public very much caught up in the aftershocks of the French Revolution and the monarchist reaction in the first half of the nineteenth century. The fear over popular sovereignty was enormous on the old continent. A Holy Alliance had formed about the time of the Congress of Vienna among the European monarchies of Prussia, Austria, and Russia to prevent the anticipated disorder of people participating in government. Pressure to grant greater freedoms and more autonomy to the people was building up. It was the period of debates and battles that eventually led to the independence of Belgium, Poland, Greece, and smaller regions in almost each of the European nations.

De Tocqueville is far better known in America, where he is studied and quoted far more often. He is frequently recognized as a remarkably insightful observer. He intertwined admiration for republican freedoms with warnings about the excesses of popular autonomy. He wrote at a time during which the ideas of Jacksonian democracy blossomed. Truth about and responsibility in all of life was now accessible to the common man, who can use his goodwill, reason, and an inner light or voice to give shape to land and society. Truth as concern merely for an educated elite, monarchs, nobility, or church was a thing of the past.

Europe at the time went through major struggles for stability and orientation. The French Revolution of 1789 had changed the physical but even more so the philosophical and cultural landscape of the old continent. Napoleon's wars and imperial aspirations had ended with his defeat at Waterloo and subsequent exile. The Holy Alliance resisted any republican influence that might seep out from France. Decembrists, who wanted more participation and greater freedoms in

Russia, were sentenced to death or exiled to Siberia. In Western Europe the pressure against the old orders resulted in the revolutions of 1830 and 1848.

De Tocqueville is so interesting because he relates not so much any number of anecdotes from a travel log or a cultural study, but rather describes a new world, a new experiment, a world created by men and women who had left the old. The pursuit of change and something new in Europe after 1830 not only gave rise to streams of political and economic emigrants who followed earlier persecuted pilgrims in large numbers to the new world—it also expressed a malaise about the old continent, where the building blocks of life would soon fall into ruin, where old authorities were questioned and traditional structures were weakened by political, cultural, and scientific shocks.

The old continent was then, with some hope, casting one eye to America and another to Russia. Both were largely empty spaces, full of promise and also of risk for people. De Tocqueville went to write about the first, the Marquis de Custine about the second only a few years later (*The Empire of the Czar*, 1839). De Custine leaves us with an excellent description of his areas of interest and his analysis of a historic situation in the West. From it we get a taste of what made it so interesting and necessary to leave for a while the older Europe and to look for alternatives elsewhere. He writes:

> All other nations seem to have reached their natural limits, and they have only to maintain their power; but these [Russia and America] are still in the act of growing. . . . The American struggles against the obstacles that nature imposes on him; the adversaries of the Russian are men. The former combats the wilderness and savage life, the latter, civilization with all its arms. The conquests of the American are therefore gained by the plowshare, those of the Russians by the sword. The Anglo-American relies on personal interest to accomplish his ends and gives free scope to the unguided strength and common sense of the people; the Russian centers all authority of society on a single arm. The principal instrument of the former is freedom; of the latter, servitude. Their starting point is different

and their courses are not the same; yet each of them seems marked out by the will of Heaven to sway the destiny of half a globe.[2]

America was then seen as the expression of the growth of equality and individuality against the background of European resistance against popular participation in government. Russia, by contrast, was looked on as the reminder of the advantage of monarchy and autocracy against the "silliness" of the common people. Yet the detailed experiences in Russia turned de Custine into an ardent advocate of limited government. Both books reveal to us the underlying currents of the two nations' lives into the future of our own time. They share the insight of outsiders and observe what even to us today seems still very familiar.

Their descriptions are in some ways similar, but with radically opposite findings. De Tocqueville saw in America the working out of a way to irresistibly undo the power of the blood-related leadership by the aristocracy in favor of a more skill-based democracy. He was pleased with the development and effects in practice of the principle of equality, to which all men contribute by their life and work. Yet he also saw that while a republic as a form of government has nobility in its own right, it depends very much on the nobility of the participants to be sustained and to be continued.

He warned on one hand against those who would obstruct in history the move toward greater freedoms. On the other he also saw impending dangers, for such freedoms could create a new tyrant—a possibly uneducated and irresponsible public as a result of an irrational and freely chosen selfishness, which finds expression in a general disinterest in a larger world and in lasting truth of old and in a failure to take on responsibilities of free men and women toward the common good. De Tocqueville spoke of the dangers of listening to self-applause. Here was a door for the weakness and insecurity of the individual, when a majority weighs in with a different position that advances only personal futures. He also saw the danger of overconfidence, when no judge exists apart from us to be a damper on pride, arrogance, and what we now call self-esteem. De Tocqueville writes, "The nations of our time cannot prevent the condition of men from becoming equal, but it depends upon themselves whether the principle of equality is to lead them to servitude or freedom, to knowledge or barbarism, to prosperity or wretchedness."[3]

He thus throws a ball back into the court of each single player. Just because we play with freedom and enjoy it does not mean we are free to neglect the "congenital menace of democracy" and forget our own responsibility for truth, reason, and morality by stupidly submitting to the common or the uncommon. De Tocqueville saw, even back then, a danger in the marriage of too much power with too little wisdom. A nation of producers, traders, and consumers runs the risk of measuring most things by their motion, possibilities of the market, and the speed of the transaction and expected future results. What sells must be good. People should be given what they like. Technique and therapy become more important than truth and wholesome teaching. Easy distractions replace earnest discernment. Personal responsibility is transformed by private reveling. Equal opportunity for all opens the door for the use of opportunities to choose between the unequals of good and evil.

For most Europeans, America remains an attractive mystery. Though much is known about the country, its history, its people, its form of government, its public image, its industrial might, and its religious roots, the reality is always more complex and less understood than they expect. America is attractive for its beauty, its freedoms, its imagined and real possibilities, and its youthfulness. To people from an older culture America is a constant reminder of their youth now long gone or never really experienced. Americans find it much easier to express the imagination, the lightness, the daring and childish hopefulness that have been lost in the rough and tumble of a longer history on other continents. Most people there have been exposed to and contained in centuries of a less privileged and more conformist or traditional life.

Visitors are almost always attracted by the kind of things they miss in other places. Of course, that is a major reason for any travel. One wants to enlarge the horizon of one's world, add experiences, and gauge one's reactions by facing new situations. We go to Italy to experience the sun, wine, and olives, the love of life and children, the beauty of the music, and the art of the Renaissance. We visit Scandinavia to be enthralled by the forests and lakes, the Nordic light, the empty spaces and colorful houses. As the wind sweeps from the sea over the dikes, Holland is a statement of resistance against nature's harsh and uncaring elements. Fatigued from life in our regimented, controlled, and rational modern lives, some might even go to more exotic places and there find a thrill in the native, the primitive, and the other-cultured.

One does not come to the United States on the way to somewhere else. By contrast one might go through Holland on the way to Britain or through Germany on the way to Sweden. One travels to New York or California because one wants to be there and not somewhere else. There is ample literature about the country. It is always in the news. The size of the land, its varied natural beauty, and its economy make it a place to see for itself. One has met interesting Americans abroad. One is attracted by the culture—movies from Hollywood, musicals in New York, architecture in the cities and the museums, which bought whole collections and with them brought samples of the world's various cultures to an audience that otherwise would have little living contact with the world that produced such art in the first place. America is in some way more a culture-displaying country than a culture-producing one. Daniel Boorstin has pointed out the use of such a public space and parade ground as the Washington Mall for a full assortment of museums exhibiting the world's nature and the world's culture. New York has its "Museum Mile" on Fifth Avenue along Central Park.

There are reasons besides mere tourism that make America attractive to the foreigner. Her universities are known for their research programs and institutes. The fibers and threads of public and private interests and funding contribute to all areas of life. The spirit of inquiry, the freedom to explore many avenues in search of issues and solutions, the self-generating interests, and the private support of such efforts are singular in the modern world. We all admire all this deeply. Any health-conscious potentate from some distant country will, without the slightest hesitation, fly to Minnesota's Mayo Clinic to get attention and find a cure. Once returned home he will probably continue to express his resentment over America and not promote better know-how or a greater openness in the market of ideas, in order to protect his own unpopular power and rule.

And there is the landscape of that new continent, largely empty still, really still a new world. Powerful rivers, destructive natural forces like hurricanes, icy rain and poison ivy, empty forests and exotic rock formations—nature in all her glory, with all her puzzles and with all her cruel power breaks into the best organized human settlement. And man turns around and seeks to control her. The marks of people exercising dominion are everywhere, laughing at nature's face and selling safe access with endless explanations, warnings, and fines for violators of safety rules to anyone on foot or in a wheelchair.

Just as remarkable and surprising, but also often bewildering, is the role of religion in the American human landscape. Scientists who speak about their faith openly, Christian literature about a host of subjects, dollar bills that announce "In God we Trust," at least since Eisenhower's presidency, and National Prayer Breakfasts are all part of a unique and different world. Not one but a dozen churches dot the typical Midwestern town and are found in both the poor and wealthy sections of large cities. Religious broadcasts of every shade of persuasion surface between the country music stations and networks that warn repeatedly against dangers lurking from the religious right. Advertisements for tires, Bibles, a better mustard, and spiritual health at a retreat compete for attention. Driving across the country one is told sometimes to "go to the church of your choice"; or more selectively, "go to church or go to hell." One night people are invited to play bingo in the same church that urges repentance by gamblers the following weekend.

Visitors are, however, not only *attracted* by such delight, such variety, such novelty and playfulness. At times a measure of *repulsion* is also felt and expressed. There is much to grieve over and to reject. The go-getter, booster mentality from the nineteenth century has marked the landscape and left many ruins of past and failed efforts. Rust and ruins line the roads on which people have moved west. Cities went through a long time of being deserted by those whose enterprise gave them shape, character, and an economic base. For too long they were abandoned and rendered almost inhabitable. The enormous freedoms from the beginning have also washed up junk, waste, and selfish greed. The mentality of a flight from the past, of being on the move constantly, of always seeking greener pastures elsewhere and never really settling down creates a focus on the self, the individual, and on change as a habit. The number of Christians who change their church affiliation in search of better fellowship, kinder discipline, or more entertaining programs is larger then those who remain where their parents lie buried and where they grew up.

In consequence of the American historic experience of migration, of people preceding government, of individualistic responsibilities, private interests take preponderance over civic duties. There is considerably less interest in America in the public space, in the life of the community, in the social reality of people being neighbors.

Communities are separated more often into economically distinct neighborhoods, which each produce their own segregation by class. Enormous efforts and money are spent on embellishing the private sphere of the house, yard, or garden and the vehicles on the driveway. There are building fund drives for the church of your choice. School taxes go only to the community school of your children. There is much less interest in caring for the public space. Few seem to see the trash on the way to the train station or airport. Sterile fast-food feeding places cater to the rushed commuter. Private generosity is considered admirable and superior, but social responsibility is mostly seen as a form of dangerous socialism.

Many visitors are for these reasons torn between attraction and repulsion, both of which are rooted in something more than just being more or less familiar with the new world. Lack of familiarity often does produce a careless response. But most people from outside develop a relationship marked by elements of both fascination and rejection before one even gets into the finer points of discussion or the memories of particular people. A genuine admiration is often matched to a certain regret that what is so attractive cannot easily be brought into one's own life elsewhere. At the same time a sense of historic pride, of local accomplishment, of the preference for other human values prevents a wholesale acceptance of the other's way of life. Room exists for a—for the most part—friendly critique of culture. We are in the same larger family, but we are sure glad to be only cousins, not brothers and sisters.

The feeling is mutual but fundamentally friendly. In any relationship of kin there is this admiration and hesitation between family members. Americans and Europeans remember our common inheritance and as adults now still like to visit each other's homes, but an ocean separates us. The members of the family have moved away from each other and lead their own lives. Burdens from the past confine our lives, and openings into the future invite us to stretch our ideas and experiences.

We Europeans are intrigued by Faulkner and others describing life in Mississippi or the Kentucky hills. We enjoyed Hemingway and Twain and have moved on to Updike and others. An almost cultic veneration of Harley-Davidsons there corresponds to what people in Europe think of BMWs. We Europeans fear yet also admire both the arrogance and the childlike innocence and daring enterprise of Americans, who in turn admire the awesome engineering and taste of the European and wonder why they seemingly lack drive in other areas.

Visitors to America are startled by multiple career changes in the life of so many people. Opportunities abound to start again, to pursue something else, and to develop a totally new interest, which sometimes includes a move across the country. The individual is at the center of his life, with little sense of roots in land and relationships. We wonder about the seriousness in any career that can so easily be changed, relocated, and retired. Americans, again, understand France's self-confidence in persons and places mostly as rudeness, the British as both quaint, slow, and yet best of friends, since they speak the same language (or almost) and have forgotten about the wasted tea.

Adam Gopnik writes about this so well and with charm in his observations:

> Most Americans draw their identities from the things they buy, while the French draw theirs from the job they do. What we think of as "French rudeness" and what they think of as "American arrogance" arise from this difference. For Americans an elevator operator is only a tourist's way of getting to the top of the Eiffel tower. For the French, a tourist is only the elevator operator's opportunity to practice his *métier* in a suitably impressive setting. . . . His work exhibits a professionalism preferably unfettered by customers, while Americans would like to be tourists unfettered by locals. Of course such a place, where laborers are hidden or dressed up as non-humans, where anything can be bought . . . (exists already and) is called Disney World.[4]

There is the puzzle of Italy existing so full of life in spite of confusion, where chaos and making a living are intertwined like the music and the words in an opera, where the church is held in esteem as serving a moral, social, and museum function, even while neighbors chat about worldly matters in the back during the mass.

And how could you be German? Sure, their workmanship has quality, but are all their people rough, tough, and gruff? There are castles on the Rhine, romantic hotels, and cathedrals in medieval towns; but the music of Bach and Beethoven are scarred, as from smallpox, by memorials to the Holocaust.

The Scandinavians are so clean, fresh, and natural, seemingly unblemished by the mess that has characterized central Europe so often in the past. (That picture assumes a certain ignorance of the battles between Nordic people through the centuries—for example, the Swedish wars against Russia, Norway, Spain, and Austria.) Yet do they not name among themselves both Søren Kierkegaard the Dane and Ingmar Bergman the Swede, people known for their many questions and contributions to make us wake up to the complications, if not darkness, of real life?

The frequent quibbles over ideas and practices between Americans and Europeans are part of a healthy way to discover differences and to think again. It gives rise to feelings of both admiration and bewilderment, of familiarity and critique, of both attraction and repulsion. We are more than tourists to each other. We take in more than anecdotes or picture shoots. We care so much because we are in many ways of the same historic stock. That is the reason these distinctions puzzle and sometimes even worry us. We wish to understand. They arise from memories of a common past, similar cultural patterns, and Christian perspectives. Our closeness easily turns the differences into a hidden criticism, an underlying source of doubt, an expression of envy and admiration.

As father in a family with five children, I am aware how much real people will differ from one another through the years. There is never really a time when one can fully understand a child or another person. My own children always remain somewhat outside me. They are often nice and rich surprises, though grief and burdens occasionally arise as well. Each of them is a real person in his or her own right. They are quite different from each other, though they grew up in the same home and place and school. They are now much different from what we thought we recognized in them further back at various stages of growing up.

That picture of a family describes well the affair between Europe and America. The American offspring looks back to the estranged parents, which they left behind when they fled, or were driven, across the waters. Religious differences, natural disasters, political dictates, and sheer adventuresomeness and new opportunities contributed to that real separation in the past. Europe's foreign aid contribution to

America in the form of educated emigrants taking their skills with them is matched by America's granting much foreign aid to reconstruct a destroyed ancestral home in Europe, which many had left a generation or two before.

Numerous books have been written about this separation and attraction on both sides of the Atlantic. Any generation looks at another with both amusement and bewilderment. In the case between Europe and America, the children have bailed out the parents and provided for them in their old age a couple of times. They came back and resolved the parents' conflicts in the last century's wars and taught them a few things about practical matters, from business to government, when old resentments and tribal habits had taken over and had prevented the parents from learning through the accomplishments of the children abroad.

It is in many ways characteristic of the European always to look backwards to Rome and Athens, to Charlemagne and Charles de Gaulle, to chivalry and the church. They are very much aware of the tenuousness of life in the recognition that the living barely survived until today, and many others before them and around them perished. They know what effort it takes to create a culture and to protect it from disintegration. They also remember how fragile civilization is at all times, for the seeds of disruption, chaos, and conflict also circulate through the human heart.

Such seeds have brought forth great problems in the fertile soil of history. We have seen how prone to disappointment any attempt is to solve all problems along the lines of nationalism, idealism, or other programs for final solutions. We Europeans tend to be less idealistic now and have become more hesitant to offer moral and global solutions, because idealism, dreams, and ideology in the recent past have brought about horrible catastrophes for human beings through Marxism and Fascism.

By contrast the American is young and forward-looking. He supposedly escaped the slavery of class and heritage in Europe and came across the waters to arrive in a land in which he could create a new world for himself and his children. As the land was new and without inherited customs for him, his way of governing and of making a living—his way of life itself—would be more the result of personal choice extending into the future than of traditions from the past. The crossing of the water to get to the new creates the picture of cleansing from the old. Migrants also applied the events of the biblical exodus from Egypt and the crossing of the Red Sea to the Promised Land to their own situation. New people would create a new world.

A glance at history confronts us with obvious failures; the new world would be born from dreams and ideals in pursuit of boundless opportunities. "The only thing to fear is fear itself" is part of the pursuit of the American dream. But while this meant in the early days the pursuit of what was understood to be a life, defined by Christianity, of educated, moral, compassionate, and reasonable people under law, it gradually changed to include the pursuit of selfishness, the creation of a dreamworld, the embrace of irrationality, and often groundless self-esteem.

Not only would people be able to fly, but opportunities would abound, and a person would be valued almost exclusively for what he could do, sell, and promise. Separated from both reason and law in an age of private religion, the right of the pursuit of happiness would become a constant supporter of an almost limitless optimism, of boundless pleasure and unreflected, even irrational personal rights. A life understood to be *under God* with inalienable rights as a person over against the powers that be was gradually replaced in the popular mind with a life *as god* with unlimited rights over against the God of the Bible and anyone else.

Discoveries about each other and self-examination are a constant stimulus for growth. We learn from the experiences and personalities of others. I am deeply marked by many exposures to the open generosity, the easy access to and genuine interest by many Americans. But my most startling and surprising experiences go back to my first exposure to Christianity in an American context. From prior study I knew about the vastness of the land, the natural wonders made widely accessible and safe for tourists, the generous welcome extended often to total strangers, and the dynamic life of give and take, of buying and selling, of so many opportunities for anyone to be rewarded and to learn from disappointments.

But I was not prepared for the importance of religion to the average person. Everywhere Christianity in one form or another was visibly present in the lives of people. The life of the church was supported and sustained by private persons and their readiness to talk about their religious beliefs. The church invites the public to its services on miniature billboards. It participates in public life with competing schools up to the level of universities, complete with social services and media.

We Europeans have churches and other signs and symbols of Christianity as well. We recognize and affirm them. We know about the artworks found in them, their architectural purposes and their history. We benefit from them when we arrive for rites of passage—baptisms, weddings, and funerals. But most people make little room for other occasions in between. We know that the church has had a say and has strongly influenced what we know of as European thought and culture. Without an understanding of the basic teaching of Christianity, it is in fact impossible to understand the museums, the literature, the legal framework, the architecture, the social concerns and institutions, and even the attempts of empires in Europe's history.

But the familiarity with which Americans talk about their church, how often they go there, how readily they invite guests to attend with them, how much it is a part of their lives is unmatched in most European settings. It is startling to hear members readily speak of God in their life in friendly terms as a personal insight, personal experience, and social habit. They speak more personally about meaning, direction, and discipleship, but each for himself, quite democratically and as if considering various suppliers in an open market. Politicians even present their faith, or lack of it, as a further qualification in their appeal to the voters.

For the European the church presents the past extending into the present, a powerful weight from history, a pride of earlier accomplishments and a source of public usefulness, orientation, and comfort. Its teaching is rarely now of specific informative value or direction, even though that teaching still casts a shadow over all of life. It is present in a deep sense of giving order, purpose, and meaning culturally to human existence from the past. For a long time it has shaped our view of things. It reminds us of a call to civility. We talk about calling, destiny, and a Christian view of the person that reaches into politics, economics, and social responsibilities in the form of a healthy humanism. Consequently we behave perhaps more Christianly in public manners, respect, and personal discipline, where restraint, politeness, and service are inherited attitudes, for it is more a community than an individual perspective.

Until recently the church, both a body of belief and a building, has served as an anchor to resist the tidal forces of both secular materialism and personalized religion. It spoke of an objective truth, a real and metaphysical vision of things in past history, against the notion that each person can create a god in his own image, start his own denomination, and rub in his personal faith experiences, much like snake oil sellers did in American history. The church spoke of truth, of conquest of hearts and minds. Her teaching laid the foundation for law, encouraged efforts to pacify the landscape in rough times, and established an order and ethic for human life through the thinking and workings of believers. Their worldview gave a particular shape to the world of man. As a result we now view the world in a rational and biblical perspective, even where a majority of people in their religion are still prone to be irrational, blindly enslaved, and brute in human relationships without an educated personal conscience.

There are then close links between the European Christian tradition and her daughters around the world. What is left at home has been battered by internal and external efforts to weaken her certainties and bleach her colors. Too often she has followed cultural trends rather than shaping each generation with the certainties of biblical truth. In many ways the church has contributed to her own demise rather than taking in the fresh air of continuing intellectual and spiritual understanding of revelation.

The first poison ingested was the Kantian assertion that revelation was dead, since no meaningful statement could be made about a God who is totally other than anything man could know. A God defined as too high resulted in man falling very low. When there is no more God who can be known, whatever is in the image of God becomes also unknowable. The second poison was the attempt to see nature and man as divine, part of a progressive and natural movement in history. The pseudo-Trinity of the nineteenth century kidnapped that view and made wide use of it. Darwin's theory of evolutionary adaptation of the fit, Freud's description of sexual drives, and Marx's teaching of the class struggle in pursuit of greater justice each expressed ways to show that *Kampf* and conflict were part of the divine way to shape the future of mankind. When large parts of the church thus had undermined its moral basis to resist social, political, and moral evil, the church had not much left to resist the inhumanity of the twentieth century. It became the century in which God was either absent or had died. Intellectually and culturally people would turn elsewhere to search for meaning—in work, travel, other religions, and many causes in an effort to escape the meaninglessness of a world without God and the image of God.

The light of the Son had gone out in the church. The night sky has only the reflected light from the moon.

American churches express in far more personal terms a religious conviction that is always very important to the individual. For him God is not dead, since he talked to God this morning. European culture relates to Christian content in a more historical, social, cultural, and external manner, often without realizing the Christian roots of thought forms, behavior, and human values that are still affirmed. The American bursts with all kinds of religious convictions. The European travels through the remains of Christianity, studies it, but then looks to other forms and content for his personal direction and interests. And yet, like de Tocqueville almost two centuries ago, we are fascinated and sometimes scared by both the expression of religion in the life of Americans and the lightness of its contribution. We deeply admire such faith and yet have little intellectual reason to understand, much less to learn from it. We are attracted to the pull of a meaningful life and repelled by its frequent and casual superficiality. The pursuit of human freedom and the conviction of moral absolutes are so attractive; yet they are expressed so often in hideous individualism and arrogant power.

That confusing picture forces us to look closer for greater clarity of what is Christian and what is merely a personal religion, a further expression of talking tall in a free market of ideas.

2

PERSONAL
DISCOVERIES

I did not grow up in a Christian family, as Americans would understand that term. We were Europeans—orderly, tolerant, and resisting evil. In our family that included the evils of National Socialism and Hitler's Aryan paganism. Ideas tied to nature, blood, and earth or land have no other control than that of power over weakness. Reason, morals, and distinctly human values are abandoned in these ideologies. In our family we discussed history, geography, and politics on Sunday morning and learned why one bit of land in the Netherlands belonged for a while, through marriage, to Austria. To be Christian meant to be European in the humanist tradition, valuing the human being, working well with moral responsibilities, and trying to stem the tide of evil, war, and inhumanity. The latter category existed in our minds and hearts as part of the Christian tradition, where the human being had been given value in the unique distinctive of having been made separately in the image of God. That is what it meant to be a human being universally.

This view of Christianity had been the fruit of several factors. On one hand there had been a gradual crystallization of Christian things through the teaching efforts of the church, the study of the Bible, and the social mandates found in the Bible. Architecture, art, and social habits of law and contracts were all the results of some people believing and acting according to Christian instruction through many generations and in this way gradually replacing tribal Roman, Greek, and later pagan Germanic habits in the course of a long history. In fact, the teaching of the church had overlaid Greek philosophy and Roman organization through power and law with its teaching about personal responsibility and grace. Europe, and later "her daughters," as General de Gaulle used to call Europe's cultural children abroad, was constructed on several mountains. The Acropolis in Athens and the hills of Rome were hidden under the influence of what was given to Jews on Sinai and the Mount of Olives.

Yet Europe is now also the result of one part of the Enlightenment. Enlightened thinkers showed a great interest in objective truth. This they had inherited from both Jewish/Christian and Renaissance interests. Unfortunately, their rationalistic rejection of revelation and the scientific reduction of man to biology and her sister sciences went beyond the rightful rejection of the unjustified claims of authority in church and monarchy in the eighteenth century.

Much of the church also gave up its basis from within when it embraced from within her own ranks problematic preachers and teachers, the efforts of "higher criticism" in the nineteenth and twentieth centuries. In this way the church had largely become irrational in its propositions and then incredible in what it presented as truth: She continued to teach prophetically and to bind the conscience of people, while her own scholars destroyed the intellectual base of the Bible as true and accurate revelation from the really existing God. With pious words she spoke sometimes for and sometimes against the voices of modern paganism—nationalism, fascism, and communism. The church herself embraced the irrational as a way to find truth and appealed to faith authoritatively or as an irrational act. Biblical faith, a reasonable response to good insight, was abandoned and then replaced with existential faith or the choice of good intentions. The firm shores of truth were left behind as one departed for a sea of uncertainties to dance on the waves of public opinion.

The local pastors of my childhood gave me my first exposure to this weakness, a stark contrast to the powerful influence of the church to shape thought and life in the past. They cut a ridiculous figure as one rode a bike to church, upright and always in black. Later it would be the priest as well walking in robes from his manse to the church, being greeted with curtsies from children on roller skates and raising his hands to bless them. Both only spoke a pious language; they maintained their form and were not expected to give intellectual, moral, or political directions. These early memories merged into a caricature of pastors, men who exuded something "other," who greeted us with mere words of grace, an oily language without meaning or bite. Later, for our confirmation class, we were told that "faith will come" but were not told what it involved. We were taught the denominational confession of faith, but nothing of why that mattered in any way when we considered life, work, and history.

My parents had left the church when Hitler's government made an arrangement with it, in the course of which assimilated and baptized Jews were looted, handed over, and abandoned. Christianity was altered to become the religion of German Christians, who fashioned a stronger Jesus than the one of the Bible, a Jesus not foretold in the Jewish covenant.

I became a Christian quite a bit later in a different context, where questions were provoked, solicited, and answered. I found people who respected both the realistic traditions of European Christian intellectual thought and an American openness to debate, explore, and experiment. They worked with questions about truth and evidence, history and reason, the nature of man and the problems in the world. I cannot remember finding such encouragement and invitations to inquiry in either the general European church then or later in a Christian context during my university studies. The lack of content and biblical knowledge prevents such free inquiry. The pragmatic utilitarianism of so many American churches today prevents it because of a lack of interest in serious questions.

It is rare even among real believers to match questions and answers, though they treasure the Bible, quote it, and live by it. They rarely urge you to take all the time you need to understand what you ought to believe, even when it is urgent that you get on with it seriously. Questions and doubt as a way to advance and to discover is considered suspect and a hindrance to faith and submission.

The liberal churches without the authority of truth, Scripture, and God have no answers. Some evangelicals do not easily tolerate the questions. Both see in a reason-based consideration of Christianity a contradiction to faith. But when answers are not meant to provide a fit to real questions, they look like rules of association and a list of specific denominational doctrines. Likewise when questions are assumed to be a pretense, like a defense against knowledge (rather than as a key to understanding and greater knowledge), faith looks more like a blind, often stupid, and always irresponsible submission than what it should be—the response to insight now acknowledged.

My first exposure to accessible Christianity in America was when "Go to the church of your choice" and presidential salutes with "God bless America" on the White House lawn or for election campaigns were common. I spent a year with a family in the state of Washington during my senior year of high school. I was taken to the church of my foster parents to meet classmates in the youth groups. I was also speaking in numerous churches, though I had no real knowledge of Christianity. Some must have been pleased with talks about Germany, various educational systems, the plight of refugees, or teenage dating customs. I imagine other churches were surprised by this "pagan" from abroad who had never held a Bible and did not do what one did in church, even though I was said to be generally rather diplomatic.

I heard many sermons and attended youth groups, church camps, and church conferences. For me it was as new, unusual, and delightful as mock UN assemblies, election of class officers, and the inner workings of the Latin club at school. I had no idea what a prom was or that the expected corsage for the girl was not intended to improve her shape the way a corset might. I met students carrying a Bible among their textbooks at school. Some even quoted Scripture to make a point. I noticed different churches at many corners downtown, a multitude of denominations, and pretty dresses and hats for Easter services. I was initiated into the Hi-Y at school. The Rotary Club honored me after I gave a talk. There had been a prayer before the meal, publicly, adults all of them! Men at that! Businesspeople mostly!

I had never been exposed to such a mingling of the sacred and the profane, of church and chums, of God and goodwill. I had never before met any church person like the genuinely interested Phil Laurie, an older Presbyterian pastor. He discussed issues of economics, history, and politics in Germany after the war with me and then talked about it in sermons!

Such is the background for the pleasure and surprise expressed by my Professor of Legal Philosophy at Freiburg University in Germany. Dr. Eric Wolf had returned from the U.S. after an international meeting of churches in Evanston, Illinois, in 1954 and spoke in admiring terms of the large number of people attending church every Sunday publicly and with some conviction. Conviction of what we did not know, but there again was that marriage of Christianity and life in the market square. By that time I had become a Christian. American Christianity overall was a far more vivid and lively expression of both thought applied to life and a particular truth finding expression in the form, values, and debate of a larger public. This stood in stark contrast to Italian cynicism, French denial, Scandinavian guilt, and German doubt.

It is a somewhat superficial caricature to suggest that Italians have largely given up on the church because she had not served them or brought them freedom as much as she had assumed the right to have dominion. In time of actual need the church still draws the faithful, even in the cities, but otherwise little attention is paid. The former leader of the Communist party, Enrico Berlinguer, was both a Marxist and a faithful Roman Catholic. There is an appeal for the art, the tradition, the veneration of the mother church, but not much confidence that the teaching can provide answers for the real questions of life. Formalistic repetitions give continuity in an age of constant change and insecurity.

The church had taken over power, authority, and purpose after the demise of the political and military Roman Empire in the fourth through seventh centuries. She deliberately attempted to safeguard a continuing, now "Holy" Roman Empire. The marriage of ecclesiastical and political power was not only political—it was also effective. It protected Rome against Byzantine expansionism. It also gave German emperors and kings the mandate from the apostolic line to extend their reign over land and people. Otto III went to the end of the known earth to make disciples and to extend the blessings of law, morality, and educational benefits into Eastern European pagan cultures. Of course, this resulted in two humanist (that is, man-centered) elements: 1) the powerful rule of the church, instilling more fear from doctrine than faith from declaring God's love; 2) a change of culture from paganism with man as a victim of destiny to something more Christian, with man as both the crown of creation and valued by a loving God. But by now the doctrines of the church had become doctrinaire. Human beings were, if for the most part only in theory, valued more by secular ideologies.

An increasingly more distant, seemingly arbitrary, and threatening God could be feared as either fate or destiny; or one could playfully bargain with him through mediators in the hope of affecting his mind. Manipulating God, who himself manipulates man through threats, unclear demands, and mysterious events, becomes an alternative to trust and faith. There is much playfulness in the Italian's view of Christianity. The church is like an honored mother, to whom one returns in times of need, but who is otherwise left in the village, while life is enjoyed in the city. In the midst of a basically absurd life, nothing should be taken too seriously and thus influence life in a direct way—neither state nor church, neither promises nor failures. The only certainty is that the enjoyment of beauty, taste, and colors has value and that it is life. It is not surprising that opera flourishes so abundantly in Italy.

In France the church has had no large audience after her decapitation at the hands of the Revolutionaries. The authority of kings and popes was rejected, and both God and Reason was thought to speak now through the will of the people. Transcendent things became unknowable; the immanence of quality wine and cheese, the beauty of women and winding rivers, and the glorious gift of the French in bringing people to politics by discussions around café tables constitute a sufficient horizon to occupy us for a lifetime. An educated philosophical elite, trained in words and with a taste and enjoyment of nature and her benefits in a sun-bathed landscape, will bring about more healing, explain purpose, and give greater honor to human crafts and lives than king or pope. God is found more readily in nature and the work of hands than in the declarations of church hierarchies.

Scandinavian society has also received much from the unraveling of theology, particularly through the Dane Søren Kierkegaard, whose doubt and trembling, fear and feeling forsaken has left a mark on society. In extremes of fear or fearlessness, with a reasonable Christian biblical perspective rarely taught, the end result is a church where believers see themselves as worthless worms. People outside the church explore their freedoms in all areas to build a truly free and egalitarian society as a natural design.

And then there are the Germans. Who among them can still believe in a good God and make sense after the horrors of Auschwitz? No wonder we do not talk about God in public, for he either has failed to prevent all that inhumanity or died before it occurred. In either case he was morally or factually absent. The march in pursuit of German destiny has been a walk to hell for millions. And the idea of the absence of God, a fitting way to describe twentieth-century history as an ideological experience, has even been nurtured by theological developments. For the church also has largely abandoned the certainty of God's existence and knowability. Instead faith was reduced to an irrational belief in hope as a principle, not as an expectation of real events to come. A God who speaks has been reduced to hearing god in the silence of your own heart, the quasi-holy enclosure of a museum, or the silence of the German forest during a Sunday morning walk. The need for rational explanations of the purpose of life from the Creator has been transformed into an irrational approach to meaning, purpose, and truth. After the collapse of two major European ideologies in the twentieth century, few would still expect to find a coherent worldview anywhere. The strength of the Green movement and of pacifism in Germany are probably more signs of cynicism than of caring for justice, relief, or the neighbor next-door.

God and truth are described as "other," as transcendent. Terms such as these have now a different, but in no case a rational meaning. Subsequently we have become a nation of doubters—doubt about God, but also about ourselves, about purpose, and about truth in general.

In light of that background you will understand Dr. Erich Wolf's pleasant surprise when he discovered in America a ubiquitous Christianity together with the open market for all kinds of snake oil sellers from religious communities representing new tribal or ethnic religions and other immigrant affiliations. The church was present everywhere. It occupied the seventh day much more than in our own background. We keep our stores closed in many countries but do not go to church, while America offers shopping twenty-four hours a day seven days a week, and a hundred million people attend church regularly. "In God we trust" and "God bless America" without further definition are phrases in everyone's awareness of some religious track on which the country rolls into the future. The Declaration of Independence, the Constitution, the office of the chaplain of the Senate, prayer at inaugurations, annual National Prayer Breakfasts, and other such reminders of an originally Christian basis for much of the American phenomenon strikes the European as remarkable. But now, with the accreditation of Muslim and Buddhist prayers in the court of American civic religion, we also notice elements of a profoundly significant superficiality.

Along country roads Mail Pouch tobacco ads and even an occasional Burma Shave slogan compete with ads for hotels, oil companies, and the church in the next town. A sign proclaiming, "Go to Church or Go to Hell" along some highway in the South hides nothing in its hopeful and simple intention to warn of divine judgment. It states the basic conviction that Christianity talks about truth, history, and universality to "one nation under God." In that context the mention of "inalienable rights" takes on flesh. The thinking person recognizes the foundation for the natural law tradition. Fundamental truth and a definition for the world of reality also makes space for the protected individual person.

Many different parts of the American experiment have their foundation in such a view of an objective reality. Democracy assumes the moral life of citizens "created equal," educated and responsible for the common good in the world. C. S. Lewis would say we have divisions of power, elections, and a host of public and private institutions not because we believe in the goodness of people, but because we do not trust any people for too long with too much power without review. Democratic structures come from the biblical insight that people are also evil, prone to sin, and in need of constant review by other men, for there will be a review by God.

That is quite a new perspective for a world in which royalty, church, and an older generation had an inherited title to authority without exposure to debate, review, or challenges on the market of ideas. This American thing seems to be much closer to the biblical injunction to believe God, but, in respect to men, to fear none. The truth of God is only poorly represented in the truth claims of people. Bad kings, unfaithful priests, and false prophets abound. The history of God's people is the history of God's faithfulness, not that of the people. They abandon God, but he does not abandon them even during the Babylonian captivity.

In the biblical history we find people humbled before God but empowered before men to warn and judge them. Even the God of the Bible could be challenged, as Job, Jeremiah, Moses, and Habakkuk did on different occasions. Only in such a challenge does it become clear that God alone is moral, compassionate, and trustworthy.

Similarly, the reading of the Law of Moses to the king and the people under Nehemiah was continued in the expository sermons from

New England days onward. The sermon instructed not only about salvation and spiritual submission and training, but also gave information about what life is and how it is to be lived. As Noah was not a righteous man only because he believed, but because his belief was expressed in righteous acts (he lived differently than his neighbors), so also did the teaching from the pulpit give shape to the life of individual citizens and through them the political and commercial body of society.

When the church was present in the parish (a county or a subdivision thereof and also an ecclesiastical domain), church buildings necessarily occupied a central location earlier in European and later in New England towns and villages. They were at the heart of the market for the souls and bodies of people. While the Bible was expounded inside the building of the church to address each person's mind and heart, stalls between the buttresses outside that same church offered the things required for physical life. From the church went out justice in civil strife and education in schools. Through the church-sponsored guilds and trade organizations quality control and market rights were exercised. The parish included both religious and political dimensions in the public square of the community.

With the growth of towns several parishes would spread out side by side. Mutual exposure opened up homogenous parish associations. More recently, the growth of populations into separate neighborhoods, easier trade and travel, and a rise of religious diversity in a changing intellectual and spiritual climate has contributed to a loss of influence of the churches in all areas. Together with the loss of their intellectual and spiritual influence during and after the Enlightenment, they also lost their moral/cultural weight and their position in the geographical center in growing cities. Their geographical and intellectual presence was diminished when the church found refuge only in the hearts of real believers. The enlightened state, the town hall, and the courts now imposed their law and replaced the law of God, which always requires personal responsibility and moral transformation.

This change was also visible during the expansion of America itself. For as people moved further west, prior to any government or church presence, the people themselves became the moral and physical implements or presence that would give shape to their lives according to the laws of the Bible written on their minds. Without a king commanding them, people needed to embrace the law itself to direct and stir up self-discipline, circumspection, and personal responsibility to God the Creator. When government arrived, people had to choose either obedience or acts of demonstrated independence.

Church-related activities are a much more visible phenomenon in American public life. Not only is there a church building at many corners of the town, but the church also organizes many public functions, activities, sponsorships, and programs for volunteer services, which in post-Enlightenment Europe are usually given to the government. Churches in Europe rarely have such public presence. More "tolerant" substitutes for church are the nonverbal celebrations of Sunday morning concerts, TV talk shows featuring the "priest" of their industry, or visits to museums as shrines to art. The believer whispers there and re-creates the atmosphere formerly found in churches. The modern artist is easily considered a great prophet of personal mysteries. National and state prayer meetings were only introduced in parts of Europe from the U.S.

The number of classes in churches for different age groups to discuss biblical subjects and personal ethics or the Bible as history or as literature is equally surprising. Laypeople's participation in such training, Bible studies during the week in large numbers, choirs for those who love to sing (rather than for some professional-standard performance) on high and holy days all remind one of the role of the church in American public life up to a recent past. There is something appealing in this effort to popularize the church. It gives easy and general access in matters relating to God, truth, and wisdom without any hesitation about the resulting lack of seriousness and comprehension.

It is true that the effects of both rationalistic scholarship, scientific reductionism, and tragic experiences of bare survival in wars have dampened the European relationship to God, the Bible, and religion. The first denies the supernatural and personal reality of God and the possibility of direct revelation in language. The second denies the supernatural and personal reality of man and defines him only in terms of chemistry and physics or mechanical behaviorism. Religious and territorial wars in the past comprise the third reality, which has left us with reminders to get along rather than to eliminate one another.

Tolerance, in this context more a mark of cynicism about truth than greatness of character, has been assumed to be a virtue, a skill, and a benefit. Not only does it let the person of another faith live—it also frees one from having to consider true and final things oneself. Living always at very close quarters and having escaped the immanence of death, plagues, and injustice from former times, we tend to meddle less in the lives of others, assume less about a solution for every problem, small and large, and all together try less often to accomplish much. Consequently we also fail less often. Tolerance has a way of becoming a form of indifference about God and man.

In American Christianity one is struck with the assumption of certainty that has marked much of the public life of the nation. The inherited vision to build a city on a hill, a New Jerusalem in a new world with new people, continues in many forms today. A solution to all problems was always expected just around the corner, or a bit further west—beyond the Hudson, then the Ohio River, the Mississippi, or the Rockies. You can do it—yes, you can! Your personal efforts, individual choices, following your dreams and walking with the Lord or your inner light will get you there. That is the American way!

I find here the background for much of what is so remarkable about America. From the early days there has been a sense, ingrained from the experience of having to be the self-made man, of both a basic confidence to solve all problems and a moral certainty about what needs to be done in the central issues of human life. Some of that is from the biblical mandate to have dominion and to subdue the earth.

Some of it is rooted in a clearer view of what it is to be a human being, and seeing that this requires personal responsibility to resist evil. America is un-understandable without the constant reminder of the biblical mandate to put the hand to the plow, seek justice, and protect the weak. It continues the Jewish approach that often something needs to be done: *If not by you, then by whom? If not now, when? If not this, then what?* That view sees human beings as actors, not victims. It seeks solutions rather than normalizing pitiful conditions. It calls for intervention rather than acceptance of the status quo with complacency. The city on a hill must be built through personal effort and clear moral discernment, to promote a more fitting image of what the Bible teaches about human beings and God's mandate to them to create a humane culture. The human being is, whether he likes it or not, a child of God and not a permanent victim of circumstances. He should seek to develop culture against the moral indifference and harsh reality of nature.

The secular version of that program picks up the affirmative elements and rejects the simultaneous reminder of human flaws and sin. Without that restraint the idealism from the Enlightenment, rather than a good set of goals from the Bible, will take over. In recent years doubts have crept into this vision. Until the end of World War II people were sure about the correctness of that assumption.

However, democracy with a free press or the right to vote has not produced a better human situation everywhere. The vision can be as deceptive as a dream, for reality always is stronger than good intentions. After a rude awakening it becomes obvious that a free press or the right to vote, when handed to ideologically influenced people, only allows the majority to impose whatever ideological vision they hold. Pluralism and the institutions of democracy require more than wishful thinking from our cultural background.

Visions without a definition of content for honest and trained minds will not result in real human freedom and responsibility. The democratic tradition easily leads to democratically chosen dictatorships or to unfettered selfishness. Yugoslavia and, at times, India are as much recent examples as Hitler in Germany, Moy in Kenya, or Mugabe in Zimbabwe.

The church sometimes also embraces some naive assumptions such as the natural goodness of people. The realistic teaching in the Bible about man's greatness and man's cruelty is too easily turned into a generally upbeat message to fit in with our cultural optimism: With Jesus in your heart you will do well at all times; no more need for teaching, discussion, and personal discipline. Instead faith becomes the means for a better self-image. It is no longer a response to the truth and the core of an instructed relationship. What I *believe* about my relationship has replaced the One whom I should believe. We tend to forget that people cannot shed their broken nature. They will always carry the baggage of being less than perfect. Going by, or seeking, visions rather than dealing with reality gives a powerful evidence of such imperfections. Vision is what ideologies were built on. People saw such wonderful things ahead that they justified the destruction of everything along the way.

The biblical worldview was formerly applied to human history and confirmed by it. It was a source of a particular mentality and contained the invitation for a constant review of the thinking and doing of people. Each situation, experience, or accomplishment contained in itself the challenge to improve on it, to find variety, and to evaluate it. Even without the critique of social patterns and local custom, each person was constantly driven to examine himself.

For in reality everything is incomplete in our world, *possibly* right or wrong, good or bad. The Bible teaches the sinfulness of man and the brokenness of the real world. Even the Greeks insisted that barbarism lurks at the city wall to disrupt the life in the *polis*. The knowledge of history as a record of the rise and easy fall of men serves as a constant reminder that nothing is finally safe, foolproof, or good for all times.

Nothing is ever fixed in such a way as to be merely repeated or reproduced without review. That dynamic has served individuals and the nation well, for the most part. Without it there would never have been that remarkable internal discussion about the morality of slavery, which divided the country itself, its people, government, churches, and often families. Accepting slavery at first was easy to a certain point. The powerful have exploited the conquered for centuries in many cultures. It continues in some places into our own day. Europeans and Americans were exposed to that temptation when they traded with cultures in Africa, where slavery was accepted.

A rationale for it was easily found in Europeans' needing people to work in hot and humid climates in the West Indies, the American South, and South America. One can find even isolated Bible verses to use in an effort to justify the sin of racism when one is faced with different people and cultures. In France the Enlightenment thinker Voltaire measured the size of people's skulls to determine racial differences scientifically. Outside the Bible's explicit insistence on one human race, different mathematical factors were drawn on to define what a human being is and his or her value.

The moral and public instruction of biblical Christianity brought individual believers to the realization of the immorality of slavery and other social evils. The mentality of review engendered efforts to abolish the trade and exploitation of human beings. There was no conquest by another foreign power, no loss of a war, as in the case of Japan and Germany, to change old and evil customs. There was rather an instructed conscience that reviewed human actions and found them lacking. Political action in England and America, accurate journalism, biblical teaching, and personal involvement contributed to the abolition of this social and moral evil.

It is then regrettable that the responsibility to do such critical work is generally replaced today by the sense of freedom to be irresponsible, selfish, and greedy. But that is more a problem of a lack of personal integrity regarding the shape of reality and the truth of the Bible than a problem contained in the mentality of review, openness, and access.

The mentality of critical evaluation is the element that encourages the existence of multiple Christian radio and TV programs, the number of Christian publishing houses, the massive variety of Sunday school materials and curricula, and Bible schools and Christian colleges. These all present an alternative and demand careful selection. On the other hand, the large number of Christian trinkets and distracting personal anecdotes, opinions, and testimonies in print also discourages any quest for real truth. Greedy and irresponsible messages speak more of personal freedoms than any concern about faithfulness to what is true. There is an astounding cohabitation of good intentions and marketing skills: Christianity is prostituted by means of coffee mugs with verses and miracle-promising postcards. There are bookends with angels and plastic praying hands; there is kitsch and propaganda for the cross. Holy rollers and hollow role models in Christian sports or businesses are paraded in such a way that the message loses credibility before it is even understood. The cheap, ugly, and plastic have been married to what used to be considered precious, important, and eternal truths of Christianity for no other reason than that there is a market for such religious tinsel and "relevance." What does so much of the church's efforts reveal of the truth of God and man?

The acceptance of such by a Christian market is possible because there is no competition. The message no longer startles, surprises, or offends because few non-Christians are exposed to it. Much Christian public life is marginalized more by a lack of provocative propositions about God and man than by the non-Christian's reaction. We like to think that the world fears and rejects us and never wonder whether we are rejected for lack of convincing argument. We should also wonder at times whether what we see as part of a spiritual battle to explain our isolation is in fact people's rejection not of God, Christ, or truth, but of what is held out by us Christians as truth. There is, of course, a real spiritual battle against Christ; but the battle of God for our spirit is a different one. It is impeded, when his truth matters so little to us anymore. As Daniel Boorstin says in a different context, the greatest hindrance to knowledge is the belief that you know everything already.[5]

The sale of trinkets of faith in Christian bookstores has turned off the serious reader. Whereas one might ask about the location of the travel or psychology section in a regular bookstore, many Christian bookstores will leave you at a loss to find the book section at all. They may only have *the* Book—in a modern version, adjusted for women, and "amplified" for the otherwise illiterate. Devotional materials have crowded out thoughtful treatments, not to speak of interesting contributions discussing God's interest in human life from non-Christian but observant and educated writers.

The visual, sensual, and immediate appeals vividly and emotionally. It requires no discernment. Space for the thoughtful, instructive, and serious material of expositions, arguments, and commentaries has been filled with other products. Many people have never realized that human life, especially in a dangerous and fallen world, requires many tools for a skillful, circumspect, and honest understanding of its meaning. What is right, true, and good is not just a matter of obedience, but of discernment, comparison, and understanding. No wonder Paul prayed for that so often in his epistles!

Public life was in the past informed by the biblical view of things. While these views are still held by many educated people, they now hold them in the privacy of their homes, in the intimacy of their hearts, in the context of their own experiences. They are maintained as preferences. They are personal values, not the sword of truth. When truth is merely a matter of personal conviction and association, when what I believe is part of a personal relationship only, it becomes more difficult to even recognize the danger that in fact one has decided to follow a personal preference, not truth.

Francis Schaeffer used the image of the castle as the place Christians have withdrawn to. They have pulled up the drawbridge and feel protected by the moat. From time to time they may throw a stone onto the enemy. But within the castle walls they are sure of themselves and their lives. They have withdrawn from the real battle, and the enemy no longer needs to attack them, for they are no longer a bother, a challenge, or a light in the midst of darkness.

What was earlier an obligation for each person—to choose to bow before the God and truth of the universe—has been reduced to a personal (i.e., private) choice not all that different from other persons' choices: Will you have decaf or regular, white or black, sugar or sweetener? Evangelism is much like the lady who says, "Let me tell you what exercise has done in my life."

The days when Christianity informed all of life seem far away. The powerful presence of faith in American public life, the willingness to talk about it, to move mountains as an expression of one's personal convictions, is remarkable. But much of it has been reduced to little more than a demonstration of a free society—people free to worship, to assemble, to speak their mind, and to believe their thing—rather than revealing a reasoned worldview, a philosophy of life. The public instruction that gave rise to such powerful expressions of Christianity as the system of government, the rule of law, the abolition of slavery, the rise of jazz and gospel, even the peculiar world of country music, has been replaced by a more privatized appeal to personal choices and preferences.

C. S. Lewis once remarked in relation to the proliferation of Christian denominations in our modern world that the very existence of multiple and personal perspectives reduces truth to private opinions, individual preferences, and personal values. It undermines the very notion that there is objective truth, a real world beyond and above our private vision, dreams, and interpretation. Multiplicity and variety does justice to our various personalities and interests. But it also does injustice to the needed realization that there is a real world and an objective truth.

We have often contributed to the relativism of our own days in the form of personal truth, personal testimonies, and irrational positions in the democratic system. The extreme of postmodernist philosophy is just one stop along the road that started way behind us time-wise.

Multiculturalism, beyond the delight of variety in people's dress and songs, is little more than a justification for moral relativism. It is part of the same monster created by private or personal views. Even if we would maintain as Christians that there is still an objective truth to God and his creation, we have ourselves undermined any resistance to the trend toward the personal becoming identified as something private. Private certainties expressed in religious language without intense prior studies on the subject matter reveal an arrogance that seems safer than reflected insight. Convictions are held profoundly, but unless they can be argued rationally before the public, they are little more than anecdotal photos of someone's last trip. Mere personal testimonies or opinions can do no more than that.

Christianity and the real world require that all values be anchored in the shape of the real world. There may be a discussion about the inner priorities of a person, but Christianity gives broad clues about the shape of reality. Personal experiences must always relate to certainty about the world. The right to our own opinion does not free us from the obligation to be informed about the real world or to argue Christ's case in relation to it.

Without a link between personal conviction and the real world, the biblical link between God's word and God's work in creation and history is disregarded. Faith then becomes a flight of fancy, a personal luxury, or an intense emotion. It is unprotected by reason and evidence and therefore just as easily ready to respond to ideology as to truth, reason, and fact.

A shift has occurred from the clear and reasonable understanding of the Bible at the beginning of the American Christian phenomenon to many present manifestations. Certainties once rooted in the biblical view of the world and tried out in the practice of life, both public and private, have been reduced to certain private views. Histories of true factors and events have been replaced by anecdotes of "his stories."

In Athens and Rome, in Geneva and Boston, the examination of biblical propositions about man and the world we live in took place in relation to an exposure to other writings, cultures, and explanations. Today for many Christians the intensity of their commitment is more decisive than its content. Moved away from the position of shaping the culture, Christians have become a subculture in the market of numerous personal ideologies. Their publications are numerous; their market share in total economic significance is known. But they rarely engage the outsider, for their product is no longer recognized to fit the category of truth.

3

LEMONADE WITH
TOO MUCH WATER

For an outsider surprise about the presence of the church in American public life starts at a curious place. The European is familiar with cathedrals and churches against the skylines of towns and villages. He is pleased to find buildings like the National Cathedral in Washington, D.C. or St. Patrick's in New York. Even the unfinished cathedral of St. John the Divine on New York's West Side is admired and seen as an enormous undertaking that may take generations to accomplish. They see some continuity with European expectations and experiences.

In a similar way the beautifully columned white churches in the South are a colorful visual delight. They fit in well with the landscape, antebellum history, the deep verandas, the drooping trees, and the Spanish moss. And the heavier stone churches of New England Episcopalians continue Anglicanism from England across the ocean.

Visitors from regions of the world, where other religions are practiced, expect to notice churches in the same way we expect to find temples, shrines, and mosques in their countries. It seems normal to find so many churches in a country that has so publicly stated its Christian roots in the past. *God* as a word and *faith* as personal conviction are part of the American image on the screen of life.

Surprising to the visitor is the vast number of small churches all over the countryside and on many streets in the cities. Whether the size of a hot dog stand or a large family home, whether in a form recognizable as a church or just a storefront, whether in a residential neighborhood or out of town and in appearance like a hangar or a shopping mall, churches abound everywhere in America. Some of the smaller ones have a one-reverend focus. He or she made history once as a sectarian offspring from something larger and became a kind of personal sheik for a splinter group. That church now offers little more than healing, blessings, and spirit in a separate but faithful community.

Perhaps the greatest surprise comes when travelers see what looks like a giant plant from the outside and then, having parked their car on the lot, are introduced to a church with programs for every age and interest with regard to current needs or marital state of the parishioners. The whole thing is a masterful organization. The billboard or monument along the side of the road announces the sermon title and activities much the same way a company logo in an industrial park indicates what goes on there. In an open society church signs serve to inform, to attract, and to compete. The church takes part in the competition on the market and advertises its expanding services. Where she once focused on right thinking and a moral life in all spheres of society from inside the church, she now competes for the time and dedication of the public with such offerings as schools and gyms, bingo halls and adult education programs. In the past she reached into the community. She has today become an alternative community among many others. Through literature and TV she reaches the shut-ins and the shy, giving experience without obligation, a show without requiring a ticket. Somewhat like a shopping channel, the church offers religion, community, and a better self-image.

The church has made herself available beyond the local parishioner with the ever-changing attractions and appeals to a people that is both historically and religiously on the move. An open, mobile society enjoys the freedom of the market. People need to be attracted to the various religious stalls on the fairground of life. The service industry has cast its shadows also on the church and has become the model. One of the effects is a change in the content of the churches' offering and her participation in life.

When church was part of the normal things in the community, she maintained the immigrants' traditions from the past or embraced the Puritan welcome on the other side of the ocean upon arrival. The church and her teaching influenced for a long time the way people thought and lived. Her word brought together the transcendent knowledge of the Creator's mind and will with the immanent pressures, possibilities, and problems of daily life. The sermon sought to tame the wilderness of the human heart and mind, so that nature's wilderness would be challenged through personal morals and an awareness of the obligation to help others. With the study, exposition, and application of the Creator's word in the text of the Bible, a direction was given for life to take shape against the wiles of evil and the unpredictable ravages of an imperfect nature.

The biblical outlook freed each person from any fatalistic resignation to the status quo of his situation or nature. Living by every word from God, not by bread alone (cf. Deut 8:3-9), explained the need to grow grain, to make ovens, and to bake bread in the first place. Life as a conquest, an expression of moral and intellectual dominion, was the purpose of human beings. For then we follow the commands and purposes given by God to glorify him and enjoy him. The image of God in man liberated him from any temptation to merge with an impersonal nature and to lose himself in resignation. Particularly after the fall of Adam and Eve, the need to put hands to the plow, to seek justice and to help the weak, to further life and to resist death became urgent and finds creative responses to life's cruelty and fundamental absurdity.

This distinctly Jewish and Christian worldview encourages a mind-set of continuously recognizing problems and seeking solutions. There has always been a remarkable generosity among normal Americans toward the stranger, at home and abroad. Curious about other people, desiring to express a created abundance and a Christian witness, Americans gave and gave again. They hosted strangers to hear from them the recent news and to share with them blessings of the land and their work on it. Such material readiness was the fruit of a biblical, moral instruction about all of life. The conquest of the land in its spacious wilderness gave practice to the skillful hand and generous heart to help the next generation get started, the neighbor to stay above water, and the immigrant to get out of it.

Christians worked according to their insights and convictions in all areas of life. They talked about their Christian view of things and shaped their lives more or less accordingly. The sermon was the central form of instruction and encouragement about all of life. A biblical view of things helped give shape to government, law, and civil society. Christians and Jews understand the Bible to explain the "Whence? What? Whither?" of life. This is a distinct view among religions for two central reasons. First, that view expresses the belief that we are meant to be human beings with minds and hands to be used to nourish body and soul as well as to have dominion over nature and to create the flow of history in a deliberate use of culture over nature. Second, it expresses the belief that the bigger picture of life can only be explained from a revelation in a text and language that addresses the mind and deals with real issues. Questions are not to be squashed, and answers need to be examined for their truthfulness. At the same time this heightens the place of man and calls for careful study in all areas of God's creation in order to make good use of life and to protect it against error.

Church schools and universities were part of an obligation, and for some a delight, to teach the next generation about all of life—from meaning to morals, from skills to sanctification, from personal to public obligations. Christians worked in the professions, for which the teachings of the Bible had prepared an intellectual and moral landscape. They saw history as real, their own lives as significant, and the tasks before them as effective contributions in a flow that started with creation, suffered the Fall, and hoped in the work of Christ onward to the kingdom of God.

As recently as 150 years ago, however, a gradual shift in thinking was accepted. First, revelation was gradually denied on any but a very personal level. The Bible, it was said, no longer now told us about all of life but contained only moral prescriptions and general indications about human dependencies. Left with only indirect revelation, the God of the Bible could no longer be known as Creator. Instead, on a second wave, creation itself became seen as divine. God was assigned a place in the midst of nature's working. Knowledge of God was not gleaned anymore from careful study of Word (the Bible) and work (nature), but became related more to the degree of goodwill, self-confidence, and personal accomplishment in each person. Many Christians joined the Romantic Movement in the nineteenth century to be closer to God in nature—under the mountains and in rich autumn foliage. They left the knowledge of God's text and rational thinking and instead turned to feeling, spontaneity, and an inner light.

David Wells has shown succinctly and in considerable detail how there was a shift from studied understanding to the power of an inner conviction, a kind of Christian transcendentalism married to the advancing democratization of Christianity (see his books *No Place for Truth* and *God in the Wasteland*). Our own generation has turned the Christian faith into something consisting of incredible lightness. Man's position above and over against nature, sometimes counter to the flow of things and very much focused on being human, was abandoned for seeing God in nature, a trust in human nature, and a tolerant view of everything as part of a natural flow.

Over the years too much water has been mixed with the lemonade. What had been a relief and delight to any thirsty person on a hot summer day has now become a weak imitation. When good intentions replace good thinking and good work, a society may continue for a while, but the reasons for its existence and the realities created by its efforts and convictions will become weak. When people decide on what they believe on the basis of what they like, what they are comfortable with, and where they find support for what they always wanted, they are no longer concerned very much about what is true, just, and good in the longer perspective.

The body of belief that strongly influenced a whole culture to think and act more biblically about man and nature has been weakened by the gradual neglect of important components. They have atrophied from a diminished conviction of what is true and what matters morally and in general from the widening separation of genuine faith from mere comprehension of life. Feelings are more readily embraced than reasoned and certain content. Convictions are more private, less tested in the real world for their truthfulness to that real world in the circle of all of life. Instead, faith and convictions come across in personal views, denominational particulars, and rules for a separated community.

The Christian profession of belief about God, man, and history came out of a study of reality, revelation, and relevance to the human experience. Today the Christian profession of faith takes on the form of the personal testimony. There is little encouragement in the churches to live thoughtfully as Christians in all aspects of life. Bowing morally and intellectually before the Creator is now a matter of personal preference and personal perspective. Instead of engaging the world of human activity, greater importance is placed on establishing parallel channels to replace secular institutions. Christian schools, sports teams, companies, and publishing houses create their own market for their community. They function almost like a separate country with citizenship in the church. They are like a package of yeast that has no contact with the flour and will never make the whole loaf rise. Questions of truth, quality, and integrity are no longer raised with any thought about a larger world. More weight is given to belonging and speaking to limited contexts. Christians, who work in the midst of a wider world, are left to stand alone, unless they can be there as missionaries.

Church has become increasingly a private affair and a personal choice and less a place of real community at a time of growing fragmentation. People flee into private spaces and new homes and leave the city. Long driving distances diminish geographical, emotional, and intellectual proximities. Previously community existed among people who lived in the same place as family and neighbors. Community did not have to be created or even discussed. Now our life and thought have largely broken up that proximity. We form ideological communities based more on membership than on life together. Membership is an exclusive agreement. Part of the aspect of the human family is lost. Rather than starting from a community of people who live out a concern about what is true, good, just, and beautiful, we cut ourselves off from the wider human family. Christianity with its universal truth is not the same as a church with its tribal truth.

Fragmentation characterizes much of our lives. With fewer children and two incomes per family, each person already leads a more independent life in the smallest community—the family. Personal convenience and the need to be in control, understood as personal rights, make it hard to accept others into my personal sphere. They might be an unpredictable burden. Moving the older generation out of homes into convenient retirement settings contributes much to generational fragmentation and isolation. The distances we cover in order to experience our "right to privacy" make real and daily community much harder.

The automobile allows us to move from the neighborhoods around the church into the country. There new churches are always changing congregants. Church is becoming more a matter of the heart and imagination. You can carry that with you wherever you go. It requires no stable commitment to place or people regardless of inconvenience.

A new and more internal church of private choice, convenience, and personal conviction is less exposed to the details, to the various aspects of normal life. That church offers a sanitized view of our lives, for it removes all the inconveniences, struggles, and frustrations that are part of a more stable and local human context. There you had to test what you believed against the outside world and in the midst of realities that were often far from pleasant. We now expect the church of our choice to support us in our flight from the world around us with a safe environment, a ready acceptance among equals, an entertaining program to hold our attention through joy and tears, laughter and light instruction. Here we are among new brothers and sisters. We hardly notice the artificiality of this church family. We can now *pretend* to be family without the burdens of quibbles, shared bathrooms, and competition for time and attention.

Churches nurture this fragmentation by providing a group and study for each age. This breaks up real families. Where church used to bring us together from different situations under the teaching and blessing of one God, church now meets the perceived needs of fragmented people. While attention to personal variations is an act of respect and kindness, the church's mandate is to bring us all to the Creator and his work for us in redemption. We may be focused on our own painful story; yet the Bible places it in the context of history (*his* story), so that we understand what is the problem of mankind, not just my personal and immediate sensation. Healing comes from God's work for us, not from feeling better about ourselves.

Too many ideas about community are expressed in various programs without a reality check. Actually being together in place and ideas, across the ages and in all aspects of life, serves community much more. Everything else is merely an illusion of community.

Fragmentation inevitably shrinks our field of vision. We alone are important to ourselves. Personal happiness, immediate fulfillment, personal concerns can and do trouble us. In adolescence we require everything to revolve around our needs. But church is not only composed of adolescents. Yet we hardly admit anyone to show us, from a wider angle, that our expectations about church and faith, life and love, may be very unrealistic, idealistic, and selfish. Exposure to the larger picture of life in a fallen world is avoided. From a narrower base of concerns and questions the wider, glorious answers of God's answers and work in history remain undiscovered and unappreciated. There is little awareness of any of the more universal problems and the historic burdens from life in a fallen world.

Consequently Christians show little confidence in the marvelous weight and wholeness of the biblical answers. We end up feeling either selfishly satisfied or constantly frustrated. Both are emotional states. The weight and wonder of God's work in history, of the truth of the Bible applicable to all areas of physical and intellectual life, is overlooked.

Such a change of focus from the real world to one's personal vision expresses itself in both left- and right-wing orientations in politics and society within the church. Both offer quick fixes, simplistic, one- or two-step solutions to all the problems we recognize. Some Christians think that the poor, the marginalized, and the variously inclined are God's favored people. They rarely see that life is more complex than that. Poverty, being on the sidelines of society, or pursuing your own favorite orientation in any area may also be the result of an unfounded opinion, personal vision, or ideological idolatry in the first place.

Much of the Christian Left pays little attention to the devastating consequences of erroneous worldviews, pagan religions, and political visions of the kingdom of God. They tend to quote Scripture to sanctify their dream of kingdom values without Christ. They call for justice but have in mind only a mathematical, numerical equilibrium. Their vision is a healed society through what turns out to be a paleo-Marxist view of equally distributed goods. Their slogan refers to "preferential treatment by God for the poor" and parallels an affirmative action program without any respect to culpability or merits in outlook. They tend to assume that pain is always the result of injustice from those who do not have the same pain. They forget that ideas and faith have consequences.

Ideas that are true to the real world have different consequences than ideas that exist only in relationship to an imagined world. The Left largely operates from a materialist and mathematical model applied to human beings and their life situation. They recognize victims but never self-inflicted wounds.

The Right within the church also has a simple vision of how to solve all problems. For those holding this view there is little recognition of genuine problems for life in a fallen world. They are like Job's friends and always see a personal cause for all life's situations. "You suffer; ergo you must be a bad person. Change your ways, and you will have no further problems!" They overlook the tragic side of life. There is no justice under the sun. Parents may have wicked children, and children may have stupid parents. The rain falls on the righteous and the wicked.

The proposals of the Right for a better world do not recognize a world that groans while waiting for the redemption. In the world of their imagination, justice is already here. We all get what we deserve. With Jesus in our heart, or simply left to ourselves without government intervention, all things would work well. They have identified the enemy. The state is as evil as the sinner next door. The elimination of either or both would solve all the remaining problems—poverty and naughty children and cancer. They propose a new and separate community of the righteous, where the wheat is separate from the tares without waiting for the angels' work at a later time.

The solution for both the Right and the Left is, in their view of things, always within reach. There is no real need to wait for the Messiah to come and clean up the mess. We only need the right political decisions. The enemies are those outside our community, foreign or unpatriotic. There is no admission of an internal and lasting problem, the reality of sin in thought and life in each person and its effect on the long road of history.

The personalization of Christianity weakens the emphasis on the need to bow before the reality of God, our sin, and Jesus Christ as Lord and Savior. Correcting one problem often results in another, much like the man who fell off the horse and tried to get back on with such zest that he fell off the other side. First, the revivals in the nineteenth century rightly taught the necessity of individual conversions. We become Christians individually. This was an urgently needed corrective after the teaching of more general ethics or the marriage of the church to nationalism. Christianity had widely become a matter of habit, custom, and repetition, not of personal choice to believe God. Choices are personal because only persons make them. Neither nature nor history nor a machine has the consciousness to make them for us.

The emphasis on the personal also had some regrettable results. With it we fell off the horse on the other side. The personal focus in conversion elevated the individual, so that the person could and did become the center of his theology. Revivals coincided with the move from an acknowledged larger world to the world that the individual could oversee. The Bible, the gospel, and life experiences invite us to seek wisdom in our effort to understand the world, creation, and the existence of God. Revivals often had a single focus—the individual's soul.

Personal faith has insidiously become married to the idea of a personal worldview, a private perspective from personal knowledge and personal interests. The nineteenth century talked about the person in contrast to animal instincts, scientific law, and an absolutist monarchy. It was a century of rising personal awareness. Individuals discovered their rights and possibilities. We are persons, not things or pawns or puppets in the nobility's wars.

America as a new continent placed enormous responsibilities on all persons for themselves. The vastness of the land required personal moral choices. Settlers had to have the law on their own hearts before the law of government reached them. Before they were accountable to Washington, they had to be accountable to God individually. They were pioneers, self-made men and women. They crossed a continent in which only the handyman survived. They had to take dominion over all kinds of unexpected situations.

Their religion was also carried with them from the East. Most of them were not pagans to whom missionaries later came with something new. They knew the teaching of God and Christ, but in the absence of established communities they relied more often on their intuition and experiences than on considered biblical teaching. They often saw God's hand and mind in a wild, magnificent, largely unknown and threatening nature around them. The God of heaven no longer revealed himself in history and through language in the Bible.

He was heard more and more as the voice within, the harmony felt with nature and, necessarily, with one's neighbors.

Such a shift is also noticeable in the meaning of the word *personal*. It gradually took on a different meaning. Commonly it marks a distinction in human beings, who make choices and act in history. Persons act, and in that they differ from animals and nature, which react. But without the constant reminder of Scripture the "personal" became the "private." It is no small step from man made in the image of God to each man being divine in his own imagination. The studied sermon for instruction was replaced by the Spirit within. Exposition was replaced by personal impression. The antiauthoritarian mood of the new democratic America removed the authority of God from heaven and made God an inner inspiration. There he could be more easily controlled, defined, and amused.

The Lord of heaven now spoke through the light in a man's heart. Yet while *heart* in the Bible is the central core of a human being, the place of all intellect and personality, *heart* for the nineteenth century was an emotional concept in contrast to reason. This has the advantage that a private view of things need not stand in the market of ideas but can be carried as "personal" views, "personal" faith, and "personal" opinions. Theology, the study of words and sentences and the acts of God in history to gain wisdom in complex human situations, could then be replaced by what "works for me in my life" and other "personal" experiences.

This would inevitably lead to a more tolerant but less precise Christianity. The dogmas of theology taught in seminaries became denominational distinctives. Presbyterians believe this, Baptists the other, with a somewhat silent agreement not to merely pursue what is biblical. American pluralism gave rise to a multitude of denominations, often for good historical reasons and personal preferences. But plurality also undermined the very notion that there is a basic body of belief that distinguishes all Christianity from its detractors and opponents. Too much pluralism makes it virtually impossible to still believe there is truth anywhere.

At what point does pluralism still describe real variety, wisdom, and different emphases, and when does it point to agnosticism and an inability to know anything for sure?

When does pluralism contribute to a dynamic challenge to see more clearly, and when does it make excuses for my right to hold my own crazy views? When is lemon without water too sour to drink, and when does too much water mixed in cheat the client out of his money?

Our age has largely replaced real discussions of theological, philosophical, and cultural content with "personal" testimony, anecdotal experience, and private views. Parallels with other expressions of the same fluidity in our culture are striking. Is beauty only in the eyes of the observer? Should marriage be defined differently for each couple according to their sexual or religious preference?

In his prayer for the disciples before his departure, Jesus asked that God would sanctify them through the truth, for God's word is true (John 17:17). But today the very concept of truth has been diluted. Jesus certainly had something more substantive in mind than what we have adopted in our pursuit of personal knowledge, personal approval, and private opinions.

External factors have also contributed to the decline in the holding of truth. Even agreement that we have the Word of God in the Bible does not prevent modern notions of what is true from doing great harm. One of these is the modern concept of democracy, which has affected our understanding of what is true. Once it was held that submitting all matters to the consent of the governed required an acceptance of a corresponding responsibility by the voters. They must be critical, informed, moral, and accountable. Where this is not the case, democracy will no longer bring an educated and moral consent. Law will follow a mathematical win/lose situation. Numbers can win a count, but not always an argument. Majorities do not by necessity have moral integrity. They only tell us the size, not the character, of the followers.

The majority/minority relation tells us something numerical only.

Without an outside definition of what is good, right, and beautiful, democracy will only indicate what is more or less accepted. In the end, what separates the minority from the acceptable is a matter of numbers, not greater wisdom, moral rectitude, etc.

Pragmatism and utilitarianism also have affected our understanding of what is true. What works in this situation, what I like, what causes least trouble or gives greatest joy to the individual and thereby gives immediate practical benefit decides over good and bad. But these are emotions and sensations without any larger grid to weigh them against. In a fallen world, all kinds of things work in the short run, give temporary pleasure, or satisfy personal greed. Bad consequences follow only after some time. There may be not only unintended but also unanticipated consequences that remain unknown until later. Pragmatism without wisdom is risky and often foolish.

Sin is the pursuit of an illusion. It follows a belief that something is real, possible, and good when in fact it is impossible, imaginary, and harmful. It may seem to bring a benefit or personal pleasure. Eve saw that "the tree was good for food, and . . . it was a delight to the eyes" (Gen. 3:6) when she believed the promise that Adam and she would be like God. In reality that was only an illusion. Adam and Eve could never be like God, since they had been made by the eternal God to begin with. Hitler, from a desire to correct what he and others considered the injustice of the Versailles Treaty, sought to create a less flawed human race. Adultery is often justified with faulty reasoning that attraction and love in multiple relationships are better than one. Don Juan argued it and became a convenient example for many. Yet in reality he destroyed both intimacy and then himself.

Finiteness, confusion in the face of too many options, and cynicism about any final knowledge demolish the notion that there is real truth. Who am I to know? How can I ever be sure? Everybody has his own view on these things and sees things from their perspective. Truth? What an impossible concept! A student asked me recently, "Do we always have to think?" Implied was the desire to be free to act on impulse, to follow impressions of the moment, and to respond to mere feelings. That desire is made easy by, for example, insurance for no-fault situations. Such a view can cover many acts of sinful stupidity.

Francis Schaeffer made the helpful distinction between *true* truth and *exhaustive* truth. He suggested that we can't ever know things to the end, or exhaustively. Only God can know what is there in all details—what is and will be; what could be but is not; what should be but won't; also what could never be. Humans are limited. We do not know anything completely. We do not know how, when, or even where the seed fell on the ground for the tree from which the middle rung of my ladder was made by someone anonymous in whatever kind of a mood on whichever day of the week.

However, that does not mean that I do not really know much that is really true about many things. I do not know anything exhaustively, but I do know much in such a way that the opposite could not be true. For it was a real person, moody or not, who worked that day and built a ladder from wood he purchased from a mill instead of resting on a beach and thinking of Roman aqueducts. He did a good job, and I can climb on the ladder to pick my cherries.

The proposition that we can't really know anything every time we cannot know something exhaustively is convenient when we don't want to admit to things that need to be corrected, compared, and established with reasonable certainty. It is far easier to say that I see it such and such a way with deep "personal" conviction and claim God's direction for it. The fact is that God has spoken, explained himself, and now expects us to struggle for wisdom and understanding of what is true in the real world. We can't just claim to know already or not to know at all.

Anything less gives persons only greater intensity of conviction, not a degree of certainty to be pursued further. Personal opinion may be claimed to have divine sanction. But many atrocious views have been held in this way. Hitler saw God, then fate and destiny behind his ideas and accomplishments as well. Many speak about the will of

Allah. In church circles you find as many visionaries as outside the church. They claim to have the Spirit on their side; others claim to hear the voice of history or to feel the pain of the people.

Whichever way you cut it, the discussion almost always deteriorates to a mere personal view of things. We must of course admit to being persons who see, describe, and then state their conclusions in the open so they can be corrected, questioned, and believed. But "personal" has come to mean the private and untouchable. Personal views demand blind trust, not agreement. Such personal knowledge requires a faith up front rather than as the conclusion of finding sufficient evidence. That kind of faith is the opposite of biblical faith. When the Bible offers to quench our thirst, it has not watered down the lemonade to cheat us out of our money.

Personal knowledge *seems* to be more tolerant, less divisive. But in the long run you will always find it to be little more than a statement into the night without an audience to convince, inform, or encourage. Each person has his own belief, viewpoint, and podium to speak from. But the neighbor, the child, or the next generation that wishes to understand the insight and wisdom of the parents is left in the dark, lacking certainty and without any lasting definition.

Left alone with our "personal faith" to hear the voice of God inside us in personal experiences and interesting stories isolates us from others. We become incomprehensible and finally just as easily wise as foolish, just as likely vocal as ignorant, offering advice not based on truth but on a feeling of truth. This is often only an imitation of the real thing.

One further aspect must be pointed out. By reducing Christianity and one's faith to what a person believes rather than to what he ought to believe in light of the real world, it is easier to turn God into an image-bearer of various people. The personal characteristics, moods, and preferences become decisive. Rather than being brought into relation with God, God is filtered into my life. The "sinner in the hands of an angry God" of Jonathan Edwards is easily turned into what might be called "God responding to an angry public." Or, stated in another context, the hymn line "What a friend we have in Jesus" because he intercedes for us before a just and holy God might become "Jesus is my support group leader, my therapist divine."

The focus has shifted from God to man, from the Creator to the creature, from the eternal to the temporal, from judgment and instruction to approval. Many Christians have turned the God of creation into their personal god, the Lord into their friend, and the truth into their self-validation. The understanding of the church at war has been widely replaced by the notion of the church as fellowship. It joins so many other associations of mostly personal interests at a time of diminished family life and greater distances between family members in the midst of our hurried and harried lives.

Despite the surprising response among professional colleagues when I insisted that Christianity is the truth of the universe, the Bible is not merely a particular set of glasses to see another world reserved for Christians but is rather a corrective that allows us to understand the real world more fittingly. For not only do we need glasses to see— we also need to be sure that we understand which glasses bring the real world into focus. In other words, Christians have a worldview that is true to the real world in which all men and women have to live, whether they like it or not.

All people, independent of their religious or cultural views, live in the same world of cause and effect, of before and after time, of man being different from non-man, of language and rationality in the daily things of life. There are not many creations. There is only one. All people put their pants on one leg at a time all around the world. Poisonous mushrooms make you sick regardless of your ethnicity, color of skin, or religious persuasion. This is the one and same world we all live in. Here lemonade has a definition. Here we are concerned with truth in labeling. Here a yes should always be a yes.

When Christians teach facts about the real world, they do not present a Christian view of things as different from another working model. There are no "Christian" facts and other facts about the same phenomenon. The acceptance and interpretation is often different, but not the facts under study.

We do not have one specific view of basic things in the world, with other views also possible. Postmodernism is not modern, but a justification for an assumed freedom for our minds to see things only because and when we see them. As an idea it justifies our confusion, when we have failed to see reality as "there" and coherent. Any incoherence is of our making. We choose to see it that way from the position of our own fragmentation. Reality is then a construction of our minds, of our perspectives. We can never be sure of the thing as it really is in and of itself. Until, of course, reality crushes us and the poison begins to work.

The conviction that we are in touch with a real world out there has been lost when the thrust of the discussion, the center of one's concern, has become what we believe rather than what we are forced to acknowledge as people living in an objective world. When we reduce our convictions to personal views, we suggest that we do not *know* anything. For then we only know in the sense that we have a mental model in our mind in the same way we wear a mask over our eyes. With that the Christian has moved into the chair of the post-Kantian nihilist and dances to the melodies of a postmodern dirge.

There is no merely Christian angle to the world of reality. Everything that accurately relates to the real created world with its deliberate definitions and with a real purpose in the decisions of the Creator is Christian. That is the world of reality, good but now fallen, affecting relationships and even microscopic details. For there is no Christian molecule and then some others! What we look for, what we value and prize, what we choose to do or not to do depends on our worldview. But the world itself, out there and created, does not depend on such a religious view of the world. Our interpretations may and should vary, but that does not change the shape of things. There is no Christian biology. There is only biology done by different kinds of people with their own degrees of integrity, curiosity, honesty, etc., as

Christians or not. The truth of biology does not depend on the faith of the practitioner.

There is an incredible lightness to the church's teaching about the Christian faith today. There is too much water and too little lemon. Our arguments no longer carry any weight. There is an increasing alienation of Christians from the certainty of a real world. Privately, they still hold to the certainties of their convictions. They know what they believe. They state it, live it more or less, share it with others, and confess it alone and in community. But from that alone one does not know whether what they believe is true to the real world. They live and speak what they see, but that has little weight in modern pluralist societies, where each person has the right to his own vision of things and obligations to none.

To use another picture, we have not thought through enough on the teaching and church level how little we actually say. Whatever we say is not plausible to an audience that has embraced the notion that "this is a free country," all of life is like a shopping mall, and freedom has been practically reduced to questions of consumption. Every day new suckers are born, we are told, and you should try to sell them something any way you can.

4

You Got Fay-yeth?

I had driven to the northeast section of a large Southern town—through expanding suburbs with housing developments, shopping centers, and commuter stops. But soon I left behind the economic boom of the Southeast American states, a result of the invention and wide availability of air-conditioning. Thus work could be done here as efficiently as further north, without the negative effects of long, foggy winters. The flight from the old rust belt of the North had been encouraged. It was cheaper and easier to abandon old places of work and memories and to embrace the newer setting of genteel towns with their lush vegetation, their cheaper labor force, and a history of an easier life.

The invitation was for dinner first, in the home of a couple who had befriended me after some prior careful grilling of my views on things. The husband had called me in New York a couple of years before. We talked for more than an hour to help him find out what I believed. I saw this as a positive thing that revealed his good sense to examine what he was getting into by inviting me to speak. In our day, as in any other, one is wise not to start with too many assumptions about the way people state their belief or express themselves with current words, to which so often they may have given a totally different meaning.

In addition, his examination over the phone included an attempt to figure out what I would think and possibly say in this or that hypothetical situation. He must have had some people in mind whose questions had startled him. Or he had in mind prior situations in which strangers to him had spoken of things that had nothing or little to do with the subject. Again, perhaps he had had bad experiences with "teachers" whose certainty in some areas was easily matched to the rudeness and insensitivity in the way the views were stated.

In any case I enjoyed the conversation and passed the test, I think, with some wind in my sails. Now I was going to his house for an evening of discussion after a lecture on some current issues of importance to him and me.

The house overlooked a lake. A verandah provided a view out onto the still water, framed by autumn foliage on tall, old trees. The living room was a vast open and comfortable space that would welcome quite a number of guests. After dinner with a small number of friends many more guests arrived in twos and threes. Some knew each other; others had heard about the evening by word of mouth.

It was one of those marvelous evenings that take place in America perhaps more than in other countries. People come together around a friendship, an interest, or just because they are forever curious. The efficient use of time, the material benefits of good work, and a history of getting together with neighbors to hear news from afar or to line up help for a common project are so much part of that marvelous American scene created by America's history and her people. The openness to something new is the fruit of a biblical perspective that truth is something worth pursuing and readily accessible to those who seek it. It is neither so far removed that we cannot know it, nor is it hidden in the minds of the elite. Nor is truth secret, mysterious, and from another world. Americans, by historic experience and necessity, are marked as practical, self-reliant people who dare to try all things and to give many people a hearing.

For sure, sometimes that leads to real disappointments, when it expresses more foolishness than wisdom. But it is also the only way one can advance and not be stuck in the repetition of yesterday, its traditions and old habits. It leads to inventiveness, inquiry, and trial.

My presentation continued right into a serious discussion around the subject of Christianity in the modern world. How are we to be understood, what are we concerned about as Christians, and how do we live in this world as human beings? We wandered in circles around the complexities of life, traversed the forest of ideas, and tried to avoid the pitfalls of simplistic answers. In America, Christianity has found many lively expressions reaching from skid row to academia, from common people to public figures, from politicians to circuit preachers and their modern equivalents, the TV evangelists and their shows. Judges in the service of law, DJs through their country music selections, and even NASCAR truck racers frequently express some reference to Christianity, their faith in God. There seem to be more publications on the market in the U.S. addressing ideas and issues in relationship to Christianity and the community than in any other country.

People are generally also more prepared to talk with total strangers about their faith, their history, and their personal lives. They invite others to their church, their Bible studies, their homes, and their garage sales. They appeal to the name of God on their money, in their Constitution, and in their election campaigns. They argue more readily in public and on every level of discourse about Christianity and her offenders. They share their homes, their cars, and their faith. They tell you the length of the days of creation and how much water they use in what manner at what age for baptism. On another, perhaps more interesting level, scholarly papers are written and presented about subjects as diverse as law and science, education and sociology, though perhaps to a far lesser degree about the arts, in relation to Christianity.

That evening exposed some of the marvels of interested and interesting people from a smaller country town, not at all the center of the world, nor even of that particular state in the South. There were a number of lawyers, a banker, several highly respected medical professionals, and a couple of teachers. For Europeans it is always surprising to find people with such educational backgrounds and such standing in the community, such reasonable people in their fields, willing to continue the discussion about a Christian view of things and how that has shaped and continues to shape the life and thinking of the community.

Nothing could disturb that interest, the exchange of views, and the weighing of arguments that evening. There were terrific noises on the sloping roof from acorns falling in the autumn winds, making at times something like the sound of a machine gun in its last attempts to shoot a volley of rounds without a determined sequence. Not even the generous desserts that are often a part of such gatherings could deter us from continuing the discussion. When we finally came to a close and the first guests of the evening started to leave, I discovered, however, that I had missed much of my dessert by continuing the discussion into the night.

There was a reason for this. Rather than reducing the whole discussion to general platitudes about Western values, humanist interests, personal opinions, and terms of politeness in social relations in town, people were really interested in biblical instruction and illustrations as a base for their reasoning and their practice. They had come to learn, to argue, and to discover a more solid basis for their Christian view of the world.

At one point of our exchange along these lines, a gentleman arose and, leaning on the doorpost, put forth a question that startled me. "Just tell me one thing," he said, "you've got faith?" He pronounced it in the way often heard in that part of the country, somewhat like fay-yeth. "You've got fay-yeth?" he asked again after a pause as I gathered my wits to understand the question.

This must have been his response to our discussion, the lecture before, and now the many reflections we went through to apply the Bible's teaching to all of life. To make sure I understood, he posed his question a third time, giving it a context that brought me out of my temporary silence. "You know, fay-yeth! It is a gift of God, not of works, lest any man should boast. You've got that fay-yeth permeating you all throughout?"

I suspect that the question was his way of saying that faith, once "gotten," would replace the need for all the ensuing discussion around the Bible's teaching and view of things. Simple faith is to remain simple. It serves to reduce the need for any more complicated discovery. Any discussion is a wasted time. It would not be adding anything to what God has given us. Therefore having faith would have to be sufficient. It is a gift of God and therefore not something one chooses, creates, or establishes to respond to the claims of the Scriptures or the Person of Jesus Christ. Faith as a gift of God is either received or not, depending on whether God gives it or not. Once had, faith has value, brings benefits, and provides unassailable security.

The rest of life, in this view, raises no questions or, God forbid, doubts. Life is seen through the eyes of faith, while reality has taken on the coloring of the glasses of faith. We thus see, but not the real world out there. Instead we see things as God gives us faith to see. We see what we believe we see.

Now there is a problem with that. For having faith in the biblical sense means believing something definite about God and about creation, including each of us as human beings, and about how the two relate. And that needs to be found out through inquiry, argument, and careful understanding of what the Bible tells us—and what it does *not* say. Then again, all our understanding of the Bible has to be compared with the evidence of the real world, about which the Bible tells us things.

Consequently, I tried to show from Ephesians 2 that faith is the response of the creature to the gift of God. St. Paul talks there not about the gift of faith, as if that came down from heaven to us, but of the gift of grace in Christ, given by God. Through Christ we have forgiveness of sin and the certainty of eternal life. The grace of God in Christ is the gift. In Christ we have all spiritual blessings in heavenly places—being chosen for salvation, adopted as sons, sealed with the Holy Spirit. Jesus Christ is the grace of God provided in bodily form. In him the Father shows us unmerited favor, being prepared to place on his Son the iniquity of our lives. We respond to that grace by faith, believing that God is not a liar or a false informant. He tells us the truth about ourselves, the work of salvation, and his favor toward us.

The text reads: "by grace you have been saved through faith . . . not a result of works, so that no one may boast." Christ's finished work on the cross is freely given to us. Faith is the instrument by which we lay hold of the content. The "works" of human effort stand in contrast to the work of Christ for us. They are not placed in opposition to faith. Faith is, as the letter to the Hebrews tells us, the practical acknowledgment, followed by actions, that God exists and that he is the rewarder of those who diligently seek him (11:1, 6).

Therefore "fay-yeth" does not replace seeking to understand what is true. There is no virtue in having faith unless what and whom we believe is true. The object of our faith is the God of the universe, the God who reveals himself in the text of the Bible as the Creator who can be known. We should believe him because he does not tell us things that are not true. Faith bows before the evidence from God and of God, his acts in history, and his declarations about the real world.

Having any other kind of "fay-yeth" can be a very foolish thing in the world in which we live after the Fall. We should only believe what is true, what makes sense, what comes from an indisputable authority. Without such considerations, faith is just as easily a problem in most cases as a solution. How much faith I have in something or someone is of no value or benefit if my faith has nothing to do with the person's character, communication, or person. I will get hurt unless there are grounds for such belief. If I believe something that is not true, I am foolish about the real world.

Many believed for centuries that the earth is flat. No matter how much they were convinced of it, they were rather foolish, even though they held to it perhaps from ignorance. Their faith did not make the earth a flat plate from which they could fall off into the void. In the same way a poisonous mushroom will make you sick or kill you regardless of your religious persuasion, color of skin, or sexual orientation. Belief is only as good and beneficial as it lays hold of something real and true in the world around us. Faith does not create a real reality outside us. It does not make a person or a situation good or bad. When the Bible speaks of faith, it does so in the context of sufficient evidence having been given that I should conclude it to be reasonable to believe that evidence. By faith we acknowledge a truth and reality to be true or real and then act accordingly.

If anything, people are much too ready to believe almost anything when it fits into their desires. But we need to distinguish between belief and make-believe. For we can create an imaginary world that fits our expectations or hopes or fantasies. But such a world is never solid enough to carry the weight of our hopes and expectations.

For some people it is easy to believe something about the real world that does not correspond to the facts. That is not the faith the Bible talks about or the faith required in our daily lives when we cross the street or sign contracts. However, some people can project an imaginary god somewhere that takes on a personality or character only from their consciousness or desires. But this ability does not create a real God. What they create is always something in their image, following their imagination, wishes, and hopes, or fears.

The spread of so many religions should warn us how easy it is to believe something without foundation. Religions are, for the most part, an attempt to give an explanation to the real world without paying that much attention to what has to be explained. For the most part they teach ways to become one with what has already been there all along. They teach us to submit, to fit in, to acquiesce, and to abandon our individuality. They propose that we should detach ourselves from normal reasoning, to not look at things critically, and to abandon our judgment between what is and what ought to be. These religions explain the world in terms of every day being normal and good. Only man is the problem, because he still thinks. They fail to explain the world, what is right and wrong in it, from the vantage point of a God outside of creation whose personality is real and who anchors our own sensitive, individual conscience.

Instead they propose a world in which we live with devotion, resignation, and denial and therefore without fantasy and hopes. In fact, a good case could be made to say that most religions try to explain the real world by explaining away the human being as a unique person. They suggest that the basic human problem is one of perception. The individual person—man, woman, and child—assumes too much about himself or herself. Once we change that, we shall have peace, nirvana, the reign of God; we shall go with the flow and experience harmony with everything. We shall float like a leaf on the river of time.

This, of course, is quite a contrast to the biblical understanding. According to the Bible, the problem is not that we think too much, but that we come to erroneous conclusions. The world of our everyday existence—the world of love and hate, space and time, persons and impersonal things—is only explainable in these details if the God of the Bible really exists out there. That is not a matter of faith, but of discernment, of reasoning, of working through the possible options in light of the unavoidable givens of the real world.

Dr. Schaeffer used to call attention to these details, which need an explanation. They fall into the two related areas of "the universe and its form" and "the mannishness of man." There is no alternative to the biblical perspective to explain these other than to explain them away. Everything in our daily existence falls into either of these two areas. We take them for granted, even when we do not have an explanation.

The first is that the universe is defined and not random. But further, man is different from non-man in the areas of personality, the quest for meaning, and morals. That is the second area requiring biblical answers.

The Bible explains the problem of sin as people believing something too carelessly, too uncritically, and in this sense too willfully. In the end this is also foolish. The problem is not that they did not believe, but that they believed a wrong thing, a fantasy, or that they believed all too readily. Later in Israel's history others would believe false prophets and unfaithful priests, those who said "'Peace, peace,' when there is no peace" (Jeremiah 6:14; 8:11). All the spies sent out to explore the land, except for Caleb and Joshua, believed their own fears about giants in the Promised Land. They did not make sense out of the situation they faced in light of both the earlier promises of Jehovah and their earlier experiences of the Exodus. Instead they were overwhelmed by what their sight alone told them at that moment.

Such a focus on immediate and sensual impressions as a basis for faith was already seen with Adam and Eve at the moment they believed the serpent in the garden rather than what God had said. They saw the fruit to be pleasant to the eye and good to eat. They gave the fruit their own interpretation and pushed aside God's restraints, because they wished to believe at that time that they could actually be like God. That is a rather foolish idea about reality, since someone else who had been around longer had made them. The Creator could describe their situation to them much more accurately than could an outsider, another creature.

Belief in an idea on the basis of intense desire or sensual attractiveness is a constant lure. In our own history we notice an early shift in what emigrants to North America expected to find there. At first the hope was to build a society of believers without the fetters of class, formalized religion, and European rivalries of state and religion. Quite soon that hope to build a city on the hill, protected by the personal responsibility of each believer, became a hope to find a new world with new people free from the sins and burdens and responsibilities of the old world. Others believed that the majority is always right and that democracy is a cure for all bad government. Some believed that the state, rather than the people, was a better source of justice than the church or the king.

Closer to our own time people assumed that what they generally do determines the norm. What individuals do normally should be the basis of the law of the land. In other words, law should no longer direct human behavior. Law should now reflect what people already do. Their belief in the natural goodness of human behavior, for they saw themselves as new people in a new world, would suffice as a source of ethics and morals. The Bible, which had directed their thoughts and made sense in the larger scheme of things, was now gradually replaced by the sensual experience. What felt good and was appealing and already done by the majority, as shown by statistics and opinion polls, became the acceptable norm.

Belief without a broader context or explanation, without a reasonable base, can be a real hindrance to wisdom. The person who believes that he knows is no longer interested in seeking knowledge. That was the situation of the Roman Church at the time of Galileo. Faith in the correspondence of Aristotelian thought with the Bible spoke more loudly. No telescope or calculation could alter that, even when the case for the earth revolving around the sun was supported in the light of facts. The Church wanted to believe that the earth was the center of the universe and Rome the center of the earth.

For some time many believed that the earth was flat. Similarly, for too many generations some people believed that blacks are less human than whites, or that women are inferior to men. Some believed that private property is the root of all evil and that the collective is always good. Some believe that graduation from high school, regardless of academic accomplishment, is helpful as a way to foster self-esteem. Some people believe that everything that calls itself Christian is Christian or that all Jews believe the same thing. Some believe that if you add Jesus to the teaching of Islam, you would have Christianity.

The quality or essence or one's faith is all too often a problem. We need to be aware of this, lest we believe too readily and encourage others to do likewise. It is not a biblical idea to urge people to "just believe." In fact we should strongly urge people against such a mentality. For we live in a world where religions and ideologies, advertisements and election campaigns, even social events bombard us with invitations to refuse critical and healthy hesitation in the face of tempting alternatives. In a fallen world especially, we need to gain wisdom before making a choice. We need to consider consequences before acting, cost before investments, public knowledge before giving access to private feelings. We need to consider who makes all these promises.

Unfortunately, much Sunday school material today teaches that kind of faith as a parallel to obedience. It encourages belief as a virtue without giving reasons why God can and should be trusted. Few treatments suggest that God can be trusted because he is truthful and is different from my neighbor, my friend, and my president.

We are invited to call God Abba, Father, because he is for many of us unlike our natural fathers. God shows himself to be Creator and more reliable, less moody, and more generous than our own fathers. We should believe God in relation to the work of Christ because God has explained the substitutionary death of his Son so explicitly for such a long time through prophetic history, in the symbols of Jewish sacrifices, and as a fact in the events of history. We compare the promises about the Messiah with the actions of the Messiah in history and know with John the Baptist that we do not have to "look for another" (Matthew 11:3).

We need to allow others and ourselves time and resources to come to faith about anything, in any area of life, from buying shoes to choosing a friend to trusting Jesus. This takes time, effort, many questions, and a host of fitting answers. We need more than just the information. We also need to think through what a difference it makes to have the information and what the alternatives are.

Any idea of a hurry should be qualified by the urgency of focusing on the essential need to know; the time element respects the need to discern wisely, for there are many diversions, pitfalls, and confusing issues along the way. Faith and action should come at the conclusion of a genuine search that leads to discovery of something really true. In this sense Jesus laments the fact that the disciples were people of such little faith even after they had been with Jesus for so long and had seen and heard many things. Faith is not something given to people, but the response of a mind that has become convinced by the evidence presented. It is not intrinsically religious rather than rational, but always the carefully crafted and daring conclusion on the basis of finite but sufficient evidence.

We believe that God exists as a gracious and moral God, for the whole Bible reveals such a Creator. We have "the assurance of things hoped for" (Hebrews 11:1) because we live under the rule of a moral

God. He created a rational universe. What we have heard and seen in the past will not be contradicted by the future. When asked to offer his son, Abraham could believe God not to be a liar because earlier promises concerning that son, Isaac, still waited to be fulfilled. Just as Isaac had been promised to be conceived supernaturally, so also would God now supernaturally keep him from death.

The sacrifice of Isaac could not lead to the death of the boy, since through him would come the Savior to all nations. Abraham could say to the servants, whom he left at the foot of the mountain, "I and the boy will . . . worship and come again to you" (Genesis 22:5). Abraham had "the conviction of things not seen" (Hebrews 11:1) because God is faithful to his promises. While we do not see God now, his existence is certain from the beginning and forever. "That which was from the beginning, which we have heard, which we have seen with our eyes, which we have looked upon and touched with our hands, concerning the word of life . . . we . . . proclaim to you" (1 John 1:1).

The requirement of faith is not peculiar to a supposed religious side of man. In fact, all our knowledge is based on the belief that we know something. We believe there to be a real world, real facts under the microscope. We believe that words describe reality, that there are causal relationships in things, and that we can buy a ticket and fly from Chicago to London. We believe, though we do not know the outcome yet in our personal experience. The pilot believes in the airworthiness of the plane after careful examination by the ground staff and others. We believe, on the basis of past experiences and insights, that we have reasons to be confident that medication will lead to health. The medical doctor believes that his diagnosis as well as the research done in the lab will enable him to prescribe a medication or therapy. We believe God and the evidence of a rational universe. I believe another person after they have given me repeated evidence of his or her credibility.

I suspect that "fay-yeth" is more an expression of blind trust than an educated response to information. At best it is a shortcut term for the right content, perhaps even only a definition of some peculiar denominational particularity. Often it seems to be a term that avoids a more careful, discerning, and grounded consideration of what we should and should not believe about anything. It is then a willingness to believe anything from almost anyone. It states what one believes, regardless of its truth, possible relevance, or relative importance. It is more like a festive banner for a one-member party or a token of admission to the few initiated, more like a mantra than the core of biblical faith.

Such "fay-eth" is unhappily widely regarded as a virtue but often turns out to be foolish. By faith many Russians believed that Stalin was a good father figure who saved Russia and did endless good for the country. By faith people believe that a religious outlook has no relationship to economic and moral/cultural activity. They all have faith, but their faith enables them to overlook reality, much to their detriment.

God can be trusted and should be believed because he is the Creator of an initially good universe to begin with. He knows what is, how it functions, and what shall be in the future. He has shown himself to be good, for he has distanced himself from the fall of Adam and Eve. Their choice was not his doing. God pleaded with Adam and Eve to love and obey him. He set them into a perfect world and told them ahead of time what would be the consequences if they disobeyed. In other words, God is definitely good. If creation in all its parts is now marred, it is so by the Fall of man, not by the will or action of God.

Faith has value only insofar as it relates to and accepts something that is true in the real world and sensible to an open and critical mind. It requires an explanation first, a context, a means of verification in reality. Faith is always specific: What specifically do you believe, and for what reason? There is no such thing as just "fay-yeth": You don't just have it or maybe you don't. You cannot have it unless you are confident that God is and is truthful, moral, and just.

In fact, we all believe something about human beings, creation, right and wrong, life and death, reality and fantasy. Even the atheist has faith. He believes certain things that tie all of reality together. He even has a religion with priests, sacred texts, ceremonies, and appropriate music and marches under banners. But is any of it true, fitting, sensible, and verifiable? That should be our concern, not whether we've got "fay-eth." Faith in the biblical sense is a response to credible evidence, to trustworthiness expressed and experienced, a response to a world of facts that need to be acknowledged as facts. These facts are both creational—what God made and how it works— as well as relating to my need of forgiveness before God: Jesus, the Judge of the universe, actually paid for my guilt through his willingness to become the judged in my place.

I would like to believe that the gentleman who asked me that question actually meant to say the right thing and just expressed it in such a curious, in some way even funny manner. In that case I have got "fay-eth."

Yet there is a second problem with that particular question that evening. Having faith by itself does not help me discover what I need to know from God in response to the challenges of life and death in the real world. God has not merely given us the reasons and ability to believe. Think of the length he has gone to explain the world to us. He invites us to discover a broad insight of facts, a mass of information in a field of knowledge that should lead to wisdom.

God speaks specifically in many areas to help us understand life in the real world, to face up to the real problems around us due to sin and the brokenness of the real world. Faith in Jesus does not explain to us how we should work, live, vote, educate our children, and relate to people around us. God did not think that saving faith was enough for our lives. For that reason he gave all kinds of additional instructions to help us see through the fog of our confusion a clearer picture of human existence.

In 1 Thessalonians 1 Paul does not stop with the sincere and overflowing praise about the labor of love, the endurance in hope, and the work produced by faith that he found among the people after they believed. These flowed from their salvation through faith in Christ to escape "the wrath to come" (v. 10). What Paul had taught in

Thessalonica was a whole worldview that was radically different from the dominant Greek views of his time. His teaching contradicted and overthrew the worldview believed by the Greek audience up until then. He talked to them about one real God, not many gods. He talked about a linear view of history in contrast to the cyclical view of the Greeks. He talked to them about a moral judgment to come and rejected the view of governance by the Fates. He talked about life after death in the resurrection of Jesus, which did away with the mortality of man as a final outcome. Death as the end of man had handicapped the Greeks and had given them no hope or meaning.

All this is summed up in the final phrase of the first chapter of 1 Thessalonians. Paul repeats the practical consequences and implications of their new understanding in the fourth chapter. This includes personal and social relationships and attitudes toward work and time, life and death. It includes the necessity to discern, to be alert, and to distinguish between all the offerings and deception of things and ideas on the market in the city of man. This content the Christians were to believe and act on, for it makes sense and fits the facts in the real world. This view and life would set them free from moral guilt before God, from death in history, and from fatalistic traditions of their culture.

This body of specific instructions on how to understand the human situation is quite a contrast to the assumptions about faith that have spread out in our generation. Faith does not explain all things or shed light on our lives and tell us what to do to honor and please the Lord, unless it is the response to such a body of content. Without that content, faith easily becomes the religious version of, for example, the focus on self-confidence in education. It is a belief that "fay-eth" in God and self-esteem in the child, almost by themselves, will magically qualify students to handle complex situations and compete for jobs on the wider market.

The good news in Christianity is more than personal salvation, more than sharing a relationship with Jesus in a generation harmed by more and more broken, or at least fragmented, relationships. The gospel is the good news that we don't live in a crazy and unjust world with each person having his own personal religious faith. We live in a world created by a good and powerful God who loves us and informs us from afar by means of a written text and ample evidence, using words that are meant to be understood. We wish it were more than texts. It would be preferable to have a face-to-face encounter. But the text is what we have to work with for now. That is not surprising, for we have been kicked out of the Garden of Eden. Yet that text is more solid material in propositional language than any personal story or testimony can give us in our need to know for sure.

In addition we do have the promise of the Holy Spirit, who will help us to understand the text, to remember what we can know, to comfort us in situations, and to teach us what we need to know. Here God is present in us. We are not orphans or the blind leading the blind. But we must not forget that it is this same Holy Spirit who also gave us the text, for "no prophecy was ever produced by the will of man, but men spoke from God as they were carried along by the Holy Spirit" (2 Peter 1:21).

The love of God is far more than his personal concern experienced internally and personally by lonely people. It involves effort, sacrifice, frustration, and compassion on the part of God. Just think of the pleading of God with people, of God running after Adam after the Fall, of his anguish over the unfaithful bride of Israel and the church. Think of the anguished Christ, who dreads the hour for which he came into the world. Think of his frustration with the disciples, these people "of little faith," who had to have things explained repeatedly. And yet they did have it explained so many times that their faith acquired a solid basis and was not just something they would mouth or confess lightly.

In our response trust, thankfulness, obedience, and enjoyment are involved in the relationship between the person of God and each of us as persons. Ours is to be an intelligent relationship, in which we grow in knowledge and understanding about God, about ourselves, and about the world we live in. Paul describes it as a "living sacrifice" in Romans 12:1-2. A living thing is not dead, cold, stiff, mechanical, or without discernment, functioning by some impulse only. It is to be a chosen, intelligent response and an acknowledgment of facts discerned among possible alternatives. It is also to be our "logical, or rational, service," which is the actual meaning of "spiritual worship" in this text. Our response is to be shaped by what the *logos*, the Word, defines, details, and informs.

Neither grace nor faith replace the need to reflect, argue, discover, and weigh what is wise and true, honest and just, weighty or flimsy in history, so that it can stand up at a future moment in the judgment by our children and by the living God. The focus on salvation by grace easily overlooks the call to show faith by works, in practice. For there is no other way to express what we really believe in any area of life except by what we do with our belief. Whether or not you rescue a child from a burning building, how you teach math and Latin, why you buy a particular used car, how you treat your aging mother, and why you keep on smoking so much are all working expressions of what you actually believe in any of these areas.

These are not works in order to earn salvation. Our broken condition has destroyed any possibility of manipulating or bargaining with God. It is too late for that. But there are different ways of working out a life. They lead to very different consequences before God and in history. Believing something is not a bargaining chip, but the only way we act, the only way we choose to live or die. And therefore we either believe what is true or we believe something else, what is false. We need to work out what is true, valuable, right and just, beautiful and useful.

When all is of grace or "fay-yeth," you will find many Christians who assume they are saved by faith but have little additional knowledge of how they should live practically as Christians. On one hand you will recognize Christians who are very afraid that any effort could be construed as works. They sit and wait for what their God-given "fay-yeth" produces, clarifies, or convicts them of. They are also afraid that the need to discern would place value on sinful man; they would rather not act until they are acted upon. They understand that salvation is by the grace of God shown in Christ and accepted by faith and therefore "not a result of works, so that no one may boast" (Ephesians 2:8-9). They often don't see the practical consequences, stated in the very next verse: "we are his workmanship, created in Christ Jesus for good works, which God prepared beforehand, that we should walk in them."

On the other hand you will recognize Christians who in their "fay-yeth" are so self-confident that they are not subject to reasoning, evidence, and arguments. They already know, and nothing can sway them. Any different approach to them is an attack of the evil one. They plow ahead with inner convictions, for their "fay-eth" has instructed them. They have an image of what ought to be and run to reach it.

Tragically both groups of Christians embrace a way to justify selfish, anxious, and very uncontrolled and undisciplined actions. A form of holy nuttiness is thereby sanctioned, and any critique of it is shrugged off as a part of spiritual warfare. They give faith and grace the central attention rather than God, the Creator, and his work and word in history. They are like the "true believers" of whom Eric Hofer speaks. But such is not Christian faith.

This weakened basis for faith must inevitably contribute to the curious phenomenon in Christianity today that so many of your neighbors now attend Bible studies, church, and home groups in a Christian context with little beneficial effect on the art of living. They may be generous in giving money to mission causes. They may be seriously concerned about their children's education. They are motivated to action by the pressure of program goals and funding appeals to meet deadlines and urgent needs.

Much emotion, growing movements, and enormous momentum among Christians to reach the masses are impressive. They are forces one needs to reckon with. They carry weight in the market and in politics. Because it is so appealing in itself, one easily overlooks the weakened content. Is there enough beef between the loaves among all of us Christians to challenge the moral/cultural problems around us? I doubt it to a large extent, when the sermons, the Bible studies, and a large majority of Christian publications fail to teach a biblical world-view based on reason, facts, and evidence and instead limit their discussion to matters of culturally defined grace and "fay-eth," feelings, and funding.

With these concerns alone we are not able to approach, much less solve, the problems in our culture. The God of the Bible sees the situation as a matter of intellectual and moral repentance, a change of perspective. We should own up to the need to turn to truth and away from error about the universe, man, and life. The need of people in what is now fashionably called the "10/40 window" is not seen as great because we have framed them geographically and notice them through our imaginary window as an opportunity. Their great need is to learn why and how to reject the dominant views held in Islam, Hinduism, Buddhism, and African animism on every issue from man to beast, from life to death, from authority to responsibility, from work to relationships and compassion. Repentance, intellectual sanity, less ideology and more realism, prayer for wisdom, and passion about human needs would express a more biblical teaching here.

Yet this would require effort, thoughtful confrontation, and clear thinking. The task is easily neglected. Many people with faith are for the most part highly motivated. They eagerly desire and are ready to do something. Yet what needs to be done is often far more complex and more difficult to discern than arousing good motivations. Few of the Christian activities in our churches encourage the discovery of wisdom, insight, and responsibility. These virtues are more often nurtured in secular settings, where facts are still seen as important and where reality is studied more faithfully than in the world in which all that seems to matter is whether you have faith.

True, many of our neighbors in a secular setting have their own kind of faith—in the perfectibility of man, inevitable progress, or the need for the state to do even more to raise our children. Others believe they are so noble and responsible that any law of the state is always evil interference. But in many other areas they are more grounded in reality than those whose "fay-yeth" you've either got or you ain't got. Not one faith or another, but what we can know and do should matter beyond our internal journey and fellowship experience with others of like mind. Without this it unfortunately does not matter often enough whether we are of a sound mind.

Friends invited me once to their home in Florida. Neighbors, teachers from their children's school, and members of their church were invited—all together a good cross-section of people. Some of them had gathered before and had hit a snag whenever the unique truth of Christianity had been brought up. Our pluralistic perspective—the roadbed of democracy and an open society—leaves us with less in common if all reality is seen as merely a construct of the mind in different social contexts from personal needs and diverse ethnic backgrounds.

There are, of course, different views on many things. A builder will see things in a house differently than a forester. A musician will see a room from a different expectation than a mother of a toddler. New, however, is that many no longer really agree there are still real things common to us to view. In the real world a distinction between interpretation and fact is always required. Today it is widely held that the interpretation is the fact. In other words, what we see and think is the only reality of which we can be certain. When anyone refers to something beyond that on a more neutral plane of things and events in time and space, he is considered to be reaching for power in order to intimidate, even terrorize others.

My host had raised some questions about the nature of truth, certainty, and moral responsibility, which we had discussed. I had pointed out that when push comes to shove, and after everything has been said and done, we still live in a real world, in which no one can avoid the facts and objects before us. Though we may like or dislike that kind of an objective world, it exists, and we have to acknowledge it. It is a given—not everything is an illusion of our perspective or a creation of our social context. We can have all kinds of interpretations of data. Personal interests, training, and background give us different views of reality. Yet there is a world of facts. We all are constrained to function in a certain manner in the world. We all need to breathe oxygen, have a digestive system, and can't eat our cake and wish to hold on to it at the same time.

A story will help us understand this. It is told in the Ludwig Wittgenstein family about their famous philosopher relative. A group of young thinkers were sitting in a room debating whether there was a lion with them in the room. Since each person had his or her own perspective on things and used words personally (i.e., differently), there could not be a common definition of what a lion is, no common perspective among them. They could debate the problem endlessly without having to come to an acceptable conclusion, even after they had tried to define the terms carefully. But when one asked for sugar for his tea and no one else agreed with his definition of sugar, the famous philosopher became cross and demanded the sugar. He was forced to acknowledge the existence of a real and common world out there.

There are facts we all have to live with whether we like it or not. The Bible talks about such facts—facts in the real world, in real history, in real time and space events. Yet unless this core affirmation of the Bible is recognized and discovered, each "believer" with the "fay-yeth" he has can come to his or her own conclusions in the modern world. For to many the truth is only what they have experienced, what appeals to their personal sense of the good, the just, and the desirable.

They probably treat the Bible as a quarry from which each person can select a rock on which to build his church, his fellowship, or as it is stated in current Christian parlance, his personal relationship with Jesus. But the Bible is not primarily about relationships. It is about God being there, about an objective creation, about man in the image of God as male and female, about a problem of moral guilt that needs to be attended to, and about the finished work of Christ. Only then does it invite each person to respond to that as only persons can—by choice, admission of fact, love, and wonder. That relationship with God is personal only insofar as it exists between the person of God and the person he made in his image. It is in no way a "private, personal" relationship according to each person's own definition.

The focus on a world of facts ("In the beginning, God created the heavens and the earth") was very offensive to one man present that evening in my friend's home. He objected strongly to what he called repeatedly "the cerebral side" of our understanding. For him Christianity is not an understanding of the facts in the real world, but a source of analogies for our personal life.

All language is analogous. It transmits the report of the facts of the world around us, of the Creator and his creation, of the person and work of Jesus Christ. But the facts in history, the questions of what happened when and why, are not themselves an analogy. These facts and our understanding of them as true were unimportant to that gentleman. What mattered to him were the lessons to be drawn by analogy from the stories told in the Bible.

His frequent repetition of the term "analogy" in relation to the Bible was interesting. To him the work of Jesus, his teaching and life, was only an analogy to the believer, not an instruction in content about a godly life. Jesus' work on the cross was reduced to an analogy of sacrificial kindness. Jesus' desire to have the executioners forgiven was interpreted as an analogy for us to forgive at any time, even without repentance.

He objected to the view that Christianity relates to content, to facts and explanations that would lead us to understand how we should live and act in private and public domains. That is part of the uniqueness of the Bible. It talks about what God has done to create a real world, in which he acts and speaks to offer real and historic hope, so that the brokenness of creation will one day in history be restored through the death and resurrection of Jesus Christ, the Son of God.

When we filter the Bible through the figure of an analogy, we retain only illustrations. Thus it invites us to copy, not to think, reflect, and act wisely in often very complex situations. But the Bible demands that we seek to understand what God has said to the fallen human race. It requires that we understand the context of a particular teaching—who is addressed and what else God says about that subject in other places of Scripture.

Using analogy from the teaching to turn the other cheek would lead to pacifism. By contrast, a study of Scripture has us understand that we are called to kindness, generosity, and freedom from the control of those who hit us. Yet we are not called to stand by idly when wrong is perpetrated. When Roman soldiers beat Paul, he denounced it and demanded compensation in the form of a trip to Rome to complain about them.

Analogy requires much more "fay-yeth" of the kind discussed earlier on. It often does not make sense to the thoughtful mind. But it is not biblical faith, for God wants us to believe what he tells us directly about life in the real world. The stories are mostly illustrative; they tell us what went on. But what we should understand about them and how we should apply that knowledge requires an expectation that God is interested in informing us about moral and intelligent life in a confusing world after the Fall.

I believe that the "fay-yeth" spoken about has a variety of origins. First, there is the gradual move from sitting under God's instruction to finding God's instruction inside us. The inner light of personal conviction replaces the carefully exegeted sermon. The text of the Bible is replaced by "my favorite text." This parallels the move from an affirmation of an objective world to the proud declaration of a subjective opinion about the world, however stubbornly held. The God of the Bible has been moved from heaven into the heart of the believer. This move is gradual and cultural. It is also problematic.

It is gradual in the sense that the nineteenth century produced more and more of a popular sovereignty in the individual. This can be seen in the realms of politics, education, the market, and social responsibilities. The ability to accomplish so much in the development of the land, of industry, of society led to a surprising amount of self-confidence. How can citizens in God's own country not also feel God inside them, motivating them and confirming their significance? Success easily makes men proud. The humility of earlier settlers before the task ahead, their careful consideration of Scripture, history, and human folly in the past, was replaced by a measure of arrogance in light of real and anticipated accomplishments. Similar shifts can be seen in other areas—the shift from moral men to a moral cause, from personal responsibility to national experimentation, from life under God's norms to the acceptance of what became normal in society.

The living God out there is reduced to my God in here. Emerson gave us the parallel in the teaching of pantheistic New England transcendentalism. To some extent the awakenings in the nineteenth century also gave us a Christian version of the same, a personal "manifest destiny" together with a national one. With Jesus in my heart I need not heed any other master.

Wendy Kaminer (*Sleeping with Extra-Terrestrials*) suggests this is the result of giving up thinking with your head and replacing it by thinking with your heart. While Jews saw the heart as the center of the whole person, the nineteenth-century romantics introduced the heart, not reason, as the seat of emotions. They celebrated subjectivity and reduced the demand for corroboration in the search for wisdom and truth. Along this track Methodism, for example, quickly becomes mysticism. The truth of the universe becomes our personal view of truth. The Jesus of history becomes the Jesus in my life. The Messiah no longer will bring justice and set things right. He has become my personal model of choice and gives me the authority to state what is right.

Perhaps that explains also the effort to have people, especially the younger generation, commit themselves to asking, "What would Jesus do?" in any situation. I suggest this is a measure of despair that reveals the loss of parental and communal context, guidance, and oversight. Father, mother, and neighbors are absent in modern lifestyles. Their life is no longer a model or a warning. Their children have little contact with them. The parents are too often absent, like it that way, and then hope that at least Jesus will go along on the dates of their children and their visits to the mall. Jesus will be there to discuss problems of adolescence and such with the child. After all, for former

President Carter, Jesus had become the substitute for a father who never played baseball with him. But Jesus would have played baseball with him!

Second, Tony Campolo used the "What would Jesus do?" teaching in the seventies to advocate pacifism. "Imagine," I heard him say once, "Jesus with you in the cockpit of a fighter plane over North Vietnam. Do you think he would drop bombs on little men in black pajamas?" That was an emotional argument, separated from the world of ideas and facts and horrors that contributed to the war in Vietnam. The crowd roared approval of the Mennonite view of Jesus and pacifism. They wanted to have nothing to do with the dirty work of the state, which in actuality is mandated by God to protect the good and to punish evil with the sword (Romans 13) and should be able to count on the morally critical participation of the Christian.

I recall vividly a comment by a former director of the Christian College Coalition based in Washington, D.C. He was pleased that his father had refused as a Christian to work in a General Electric Company ammunitions plant during the Great Depression. I countered that as a German I was pleased that not all Christians had done that and thus were able to contribute to the defeat of Nazism and its immoral ideology and practices. The gentleman swallowed in surprise and then suggested that non-Christians could do war preparations. His father had wanted to keep his hands clean in the dirty business of using the sword to punish evil. But that is impossible. Those who danced through the night in Nazi festivities while Jews and others were dragged to their death outside can only weep at such personal faith of some Christians.

Such a view is too facile. Jesus is not the model we seek to copy at all times. We do not know what he would have done in this or that specific situation. We are not given a list of model actions. He never was a model partner to our intimacies or those of Adam and Eve. He does not show us how to be married. He does not want our lives to be modeled on his unique calling to be the Lamb of God. His instruction is through words and actions, which need to be understood as more than single events or detailed prescriptions. They are statements of truth about God and man, about life, about history and responsibility. From them we are told to seek wisdom, not specific modeled direction for every eventuality.

The Bible invites us to believe God. He exists and truthfully reveals himself to help us understand our situation, origin, purpose, and present need. We should not believe too quickly in the crowded town square with its many voices, religions, and ideologies. There is little to worry about when people do not believe too readily. People, whether children or adults, believe all too readily all kinds of false and deceptive propositions. That explains the wide acceptance of the irrational, the esoteric, and the anecdotal as a criterion of truth. The sorting of the offers, the necessary distinction between what is true and what is merely believed, takes time to discern. We should not be alarmed when children, friends, or others do not simply believe. In fact, we should warn them against all manner of carelessness. People have always believed all kind of things that have no relationship to the real world around us. Yet in the end the facts of that created reality will always speak louder to an honest person than any visions, imaginations, and beliefs. Then the truth will be unveiled from the clouds and sounds of the present confusion.

5

ALL FAITHS AND
ANY BUDGET

We had left Dallas earlier to drive south for our next appointment. The rush-hour traffic was primarily going the other way, and our road was open. It was a wonderful morning, full of light over a flat horizon. The weather and the landscape reminded me strongly of scenes in *Giant* with James Dean and *Paris, Texas* by Wim Wenders. The presence of man is always startling in the open space of a large land in his struggles to be master of his life. He seems to be so small or even lost in a larger, and largely unfriendly, cosmos, unless he has managed to impose himself and thereby resist oblivion.

With the use of his mind, the human being has survived natural handicaps. He has terraced the land, dug wells, crossed oceans, and transplanted organs. The human presence alters the landscape more than any tree, mountain, or river does. I am not complaining about this. I am not even lamenting this or wishing it were not so. In fact, all life interferes with all other life. As soon as you have chemical reactions, as when a plant, for instance, dissolves dirt and absorbs moisture or when a human being labors, eats, and breathes, we have a reality of change due to life itself. The mandate to man to subdue the earth and to multiply, to have dominion and to create, to study and improve creation, and to make a name for himself as the creature in the image of the Creator God implies real life, real purpose, and real change.

America is a land of enormous space. Visible electric wires, rail-road service, multitudes of gas stations and heavy trucks, and the love of the automobile testify to past and present efforts to cover distances—the road ahead, the pit stops along the way, the cloverleaf intersections like ribbons on a gift-wrapped package. The small towns each have a contained life of their own tucked away behind low and uneven walls of frontage businesses, which protect the older centers from being entered by outsiders until the old life itself is unhappily abandoned by former residents who sought their life elsewhere. It is a sight I have only otherwise experienced in Africa and Australia, both continents similarly underpopulated over large stretches. Perhaps Russia's Siberia would also fit this picture, but there are few roads to let you leave town and see the big picture.

We had just passed along the edge of a bigger agglomeration, a college town with its restaurants, service stations, discount outlets, and food joints. About five miles south of town a sign on the left suddenly attracted my attention. We had come into the area of "clean industries," those low modern buildings that house various services—for example, tire distributors. One building advertised the "Witch Equipment Company." I assume it was the name of the company distributing tools and machinery, not meeting the professional needs of witches.

Then a cemetery advertised, "We serve every faith and any budget." Almost immediately next to it stood the building of a church that gave its name as "Victory Fellowship" and announced its character and calling: "The City-reaching Church."

I did not stop then and therefore know nothing more about the church and make no judgment about it. But the signs in succession and in that neighborhood did make me wonder whether the nature and content of such advertisements affect the life and teaching of the church. The church competes in form and presence with such neighbors and the exposition of their wares. But have we ever thought how much the public driving by like I did find it more plausible to expect little more in church than another business activity or dance studio or service center? The "church-of-your-choice" of the 1950s has become one more "service center" among others. Needs in such different areas as car parts, home decoration, equipment rentals, and workouts in a gym are satisfied just as readily and in the same location as a person's need for religion, fellowship, and morals.

We easily forget how much church and its teaching from the Bible up to the recent past shaped our thinking, practices, and values both in Europe and America. The church then was so much the center of the life of a community. From here went out the preaching of God's Word, which transformed the life of a renewed body of people. Their thoughts and habits were constantly under the scrutiny of Christian instruction. From a more biblical view of things flowed a gradual discovery of biblical ethics in all areas of life. This discovery then resulted in personal moral and intellectual obligations in practice, in both work and art, in human affirmation, and in efforts to resist evil.

The church encouraged education. The church started many of the early universities in Europe after the thirteenth century. The same was again the case in America five hundred years later. The purpose was to expand the insights of Scripture, the word of the Creator, into every area of human activity.

The church also occupied the seat of justice. From here went out the rule of law for society and the market. For centuries the fountain in the town square of Lausanne, Switzerland, has been decorated with a tall statue of Justice, her eyes blindfolded, the scales weighing the cases and her sword drawn to impose justice from above. It applies to all personages under the rim of her skirt equally: traders and rulers, men and women, secular and religious powers. It shows that justice is not a matter of power, but of truth that applies to all people equally. These ideas are also expressed in Lausanne in the painting by Paul Robert on the stairwell of the Swiss Supreme Court. Justice there instructs the judges from an open book, the Word of God.

From biblical law arose the demand for two corroborating witnesses in court cases or the command not to bear false witness against one's neighbor. Christianity always taught the importance to live in the real world, not to escape it into spiritual separateness. Salvation was a moral concern. Man's problem was wrong thinking and doing, for which one needed to be forgiven by God. Man was never to become something other than what a human being is from creation on. There was no calling to become angels, for instance, or to seek detachment from the real world as Buddhism teaches. Those who sat on high pillars to pray from a position above the earth and close to heaven were more influenced by Plato in Greek philosophy and later by Muslim mysticism than by Jesus.

From this foundation in Scripture, history, and the Word of God, the church watched over measures and weights in the market surrounding her building. Stalls and craftsmen's shops were constructed between her buttresses. Bonne, a little town just outside Geneva, has a covered marketplace. Century-old oak trunks and beams support the roof. Incorporated into the sidewall are four granite blocks carefully carved out like bowls, each of a different size. On the side a wooden gate lets the grain, once measured by volume to correspond to the norms, fall into waiting sacks or bags. A shekel is to be a shekel, and the church would watch over such fairness.

The church also instituted a system of quality controls through the establishment of trade guilds and regulated access to markets. Sometimes, in excess, she even determined prices and forbade interest for loans, leaving that particular business to be provided by non-Christians—i.e., European Jews. No wonder that those individuals then often developed a certain expertise in that line and drew the envy of those who resented not being themselves as clever from lack of practice and mistaken humility. The Reformers later took a far more measured approach when they suggested that the prohibition in the Bible against usury was not against investments, loans, and profit but insisted on sharing both gain and loss among investors and entrepreneurs.

In many other ways the church, responsible for the teaching of Christianity and the Bible, was the main occupant of the market in the center of life. Admittedly, that was not always only a benefit. Such a power can be a blessing or a curse, depending on whether truth or falsehood is taught, whether honesty or deception is practiced. The history of Christendom in Europe is a history of good and bad. The comparison between various views and practices was not always encouraged. Yet the remarkable facts remain that Europe became something different from what original Slavs, Lombards, Vandals, Saxons, Goths, Huns, and other tribes would have produced from the continued practice of their indigenous tribal customs. Paul's two weeks of teaching in Thessalonica and Athens and later the work of those who followed him to France, Ireland, and Spain would gradually change all that and replace idols with the living God, a cyclical and fatalistic history into a linear one, and a world exposed to whatever powers that be into one under the moral judgment of God.

Steady teaching from the Bible challenged all that over many generations and with many ups and downs. Yet it produced in fact a different view of the world, of the place of human beings in nature, and of life against death. It gave the impetus for the rule of law in distinction to the fear of power. The Bible opened the window to a view of life as specifically valuable and the individual as unique, whose mind should be used for social, economic, and cultural changes toward a more humane situation. David Gress brings out these and other points in the book *From Plato to NATO*.[6] He shows that the Western world is not merely the result of lofty ideas about democracy, the individual, and the rule of law found in Greek and Roman sources. Instead the acceptance of the Word of God (the Bible) opened people's eyes to a different view of things and changed their practices quite effectively and in a profound way over time.

Even the Protestant Reformation stands in that continuity with a desire for reform, not a replacement of Roman Catholic emphasis. It brought the teaching of Christianity back to its roots in the Bible, after distortions and pollutions had crept in during the political and humanistic efforts of the Church of Rome in preceding centuries. These had in the core changed the view of final authority from God to the teaching of the church. They had also made access to the text of the Bible more difficult to the common man, who was considered to be less spiritual and unable to understand it, when the church set up all kinds of things as mysteries of the faith that had little or nothing to do with what had been a straightforward reading of the biblical text.

The teaching of the priesthood of all believers from the Bible, once again taught and enforced in the Reformation, was a helpful rediscovery and addition. For the text then was acknowledged as the final authority. Even the men in Rome had to be subject to it. That text demands careful evaluation and recognition of true and false prophets, fair and unfair judges, faithful and unfaithful priests, and good and bad government. Later the American national experiment showed both a positive and a negative effect, when this mandate to encourage the good and to prevent the evil in human activity was carried out.

The Bible places authority in God's Word, not in a human institution. The authority is given back to the author, God. The church herself is the work of God and called by him. She is not the creator of God's Word through her wisdom and suffering. Instead she, and men generally, are to live by the Word of God. God, not any man, is the author and final interpreter of it. It is not justified, as is sometimes done today, to suggest that the Reformers were against all authority when they rejected Rome's right to determine theology. They only rejected the assumed authority of the church's teaching. They trusted God to have given us his Word and did not, as it is alleged, only build on their own findings.

On this foundation they could take their stand even when it came out against the "traditional" teaching of the church. Both Roman Catholics and Eastern Orthodox circles bring this up to accuse Protestants (and Jews, incidentally) and then explain their final reliance on the community of the church as a more reliable authority than the text. The text does not change, while in both Roman Catholic and Orthodox communities numerous changes have been introduced in the course of the centuries in diversion from the text. Their claimed authority made it difficult to challenge them.

Any authority that does not encourage review from a larger frame of reference, such as creation (the world around us) or reasonable consistency, can easily get away with seemingly powerful pronouncements of its own exclusive authority. That is so for individuals and for established institutions. It becomes a kind of circular empowerment and does not guarantee against heresy parading as truth, since the possibility of heresy is not readily admitted by anyone claiming elitist or exclusive insights. There is danger in assuming that one's personal views or any institution's concerted understanding alone are pure when there is no standard outside against which to measure things. Without a comparison any variant can of course be declared true and its opposite be heretical in some form or other.

This mentality also supports modern denominationalism as a habit, with quite tragic results. Here also it comes out of the refusal to bow to anything larger than my personal or our traditional and communal experiences, insights, and needs. The denominational creeds, authors, and traditions are more often referred to and relied upon than Scripture, the real world, or reasonable analysis.

The Reformers understood this. They engaged in a critical evaluation of traditional teaching as a requirement on one hand and submitted their own views to the authority of Scripture on the other. They were open to debates, even if at times these did not take place in a kind spirit. It is just not true that they were antiauthoritarian. They were in search of a more reliable tradition than that invented by religious men in the flow of time. They went back to the text itself. They understood that we don't live in a good world of honest people, where anything claimed should be readily believed. They taught that faith, to be worth anything and to be biblical faith, has to have a definition and a basis. That faith spoke about real life, real history, and real reasoning and could therefore be exposed to challenges from these. Their confidence was that it would stand because it was true.

There is no value in faith alone without a basis in fact. It is make-believe, which merely produces fear, limitations, and an assumption of being right. Such faith is ignorant and foolish and of no benefit to anyone. Faith is rather the confidence that what I do not now see can be believed on the basis of what I have seen, do know, and can expect in objective reality. It is not the affirmation of something unfounded. No matter how much you believe your neighbors to be harmless, you would be a fool to keep your home open without first examining their values and life. You may have moved near a den of robbers.

Prime Minister Chamberlain of Great Britain was naive and foolish to believe in Munich in 1938 that just because Hitler was European, he would behave like a gentleman. An agreement is always only as good as the parties agreeing to it. Good intentions do not make another person good.

In the heart of Texas signs made me reflect on things of greater contemporary interest. What commercial interest might have driven the administrator of a cemetery to advertise that they served all faiths and any budget? That is an invitation one can't refuse. I imagine it was a statement of variety, in recognition of a common human need and fundamental agreement about burials. It reflects a practical and commercial interest in satisfying real needs, a willingness to transcend denominational barriers, a more tolerant approach to former customs. Previously only special spaces outside the holy ground of the denominational cemeteries were made available for infidels of whatever other group than their own. People who had committed suicide and corpses of unknown folk found in fields and forests were also buried there. Better things were reserved only for the unknown soldier.

In Texas people are invited to put all these distinctions aside. Commercial interests overcome all religious distinctions. When my father came back from his first trip to America, he was full of wonderful and oft-repeated stories. One of the memorable ones was about the sign outside a hotel room window. From morning to late evening he could read in bright colors the sign for a funeral parlor next-door: "You just die. We do the rest." In other words, the body has served its purpose. Let it now be disposed of by us in a worry-free way. No one is excluded. Neither a particular religion nor budget should matter. In death we are fully equal. Let priests and relations say anything they want, let it be a pine box or a mausoleum, let it be the return to nature or the will of God!

Books have been written about the variety of funeral practices in America. The actions of Forest Lawn (in California) and other famous ceremonies comprise a recognized phenomenon for the pretense of eternal life in a sanitized funeral setting with lasting pleasant memories, good music of your choice, and a setting of eternal springtime and lawn picnics. In the disposal of your body, your personal faith no longer matters. Faith and price are no hindrance in a funeral.

I imagine, of course, that a believing Hindu would not be allowed to practice suttee or widow burning on the funeral pyre in America. There are limits to "all faiths," for the assumption is that whatever faith people have will conform to some of the basic things for which Christianity alone gives a foundation. But maybe it does include Mormons and Jehovah's Witnesses and Christian Scientists, all American inventions of pseudo-Christian alternatives for which the openness of the land in the nineteenth century had enough space, curiosity, and indifference. Like snake oil and other fantasies, a multitude of religions and utopian communities could be sold to a public that expected unlimited opportunities and unimaginable surprises in a totally new land.

Yet some limits do exist at times even in cemeteries. Valhalla, New York, is a curious town at the base of a water reservoir just north of New York City. It is named after the wish of the local postmistress many years ago who, as an admirer of Richard Wagner's music, wanted the railroad station named after the Norse mythical place of the dead in battle, Valhalla. A number of extensive cemeteries line the valley along the commuter tracks. A huge stone gate gives the name of one of them: "Heaven's Gate." This needs no further definition or specification in our modern day, where religious myth deals with souls, while material bodies get burned or belong in the ground. But then, as if to show that this thing about "Heaven" should not be taken too seriously by people in the twentieth century, a smaller sign at the base of the stone arch reads, "Gate closes at 5 PM."

Almost next to the cemetery for all faiths and any budget in Texas, about five miles out of town, stood the sign for a church fellowship that promised to be a "city-reaching church." The sign of this fellowship announced a mission, gave a program, expressed aspiration, and directed the work of believers. It did not describe or relate to the present geography of the location. These words may have been tall talk. A hoped-for situation was presented long enough to make it come true, because people would believe it. The Texas town might just expand along its highways and at some future date include that church building. At such time it will have become a church that could be reaching the city with its work. But for the moment it existed outside of town, a place and building that drew people away from town.

That location, and that of many other newer church buildings, shows how much the church exists more as a central idea to believers, not an important reality in the civic, geographical, and even moral life of a people. The city-reaching church can exist outside the city. Its members may have such an outreach in mind, but it is more a fiction than a reality. It reaches the city in the minds of the members, reaching out to other minds. The modern mobility, the ease of travel for like-minded people, made this church possible at the end of a long commute outside of the city.

At churches like this people come from far away for the purpose of being a community of emotions and ideas, regardless of their distant lives and the inconvenience of getting together. Their life is little involved in all the aspects of the city. There is no way to meet often except by phone or a long drive. It is a spiritual community, rarely one with intellectual, cultural, and material consequences. There is little weight to it. The only contact is the one created for a moment. There is little crossing of paths, no neighborhood, no public expression and reminder of the truth proclaimed, no common voice, no powerful presence. When the church is located out of town, there is no silent witness even. Church has become more of an inner idea, a deep and shared conviction, but not a demonstrable reality to be respected by other parts of the life of a city.

Of course, the church is foremost a body of believers. The building is a later convenience and the result of such a community. The life of the church is found in an accepted biblical view of the world, which includes love, large areas of moral and artistic agreement, and genuine human relationships across generations. It includes an ethic of the nobility of work and lawful governance. All these parts result in the practical responsibilities of people. But at a certain point in time the building and other practical forms of what is believed about all of life should take on a significance that supports, in external terms, the content of the ideas embraced by the people. If they believe in a rational and good God, their work and thought should express that. If they believe in a creative, good, and powerful God, their lives and work should be able to express creativity, thought, goodness, and determination. When they believe that man is made in the image of God, the life of the church should express that in real terms in the life of society across every field of human existence.

That view found expression in the cathedrals of Europe and the churches in New England in their attempts to speak into the external world around them with objects, color and form, location and variety about the understanding of God and man, which the people inside believed. For they believed something not merely in their hearts or related to eternity, but they believed something about the truth of the universe, with practical and ethical consequences in the world around them. The core of their lives was not a personal relationship with Jesus but rather a personal submission in all of life to the truth of God's real and communicated existence.

With that understanding they not only reached into the city— they became the core of the city, as I suggested earlier. The city formed around them as they nurtured it, admonished it, worked and played in it, sought and administered justice, and gave protection and dignity to the human being made in the image of God. The city was not a statement of revolt against God, as Jacques Ellul believed, but always a mixture of good and bad choices by people. The city was always an encouragement from what people could do. At the same time it contained a warning about what evil government could produce.

Yet overall when the church of believers believed what Scripture told her, she became salt and light and raised the beacon, figuratively speaking, all the way to the top of the steeple.

Only under the influence of ideological liberalism and what is called scientific theology in the nineteenth century did the lights go out, and trees reaching into the sky took the place of the church tower. The Dutch painter Van Gogh gives that such vivid expression in his famous painting "The Starry Night." Now the church windows are dark. Cypress trees make the connection with what remains of heaven. There are wildly swirling clouds with the light of the moon and stars. Christians have often contributed to this decline in the public presence and in the ministry of the church by hiding the truth in the folds and chambers of their hearts. They keep it in the form of profoundly held and oft-repeated convictions without having to pass muster in the open intellectual battles further out. Other forces consequently occupied the intellectual and moral territory, those of the market, of sensual temptations and the distractions found in novelty alone and the exotic.

Much of Christianity is heard today merely as a set of private ideas, a set of opinions freely held, at most a voting bloc across precinct lines. It is rarely experienced as a living reality of neighborhoods, of real issues raised intelligently in public debates, where the sanity of a humane worldview reaches into the warp and woof of a civic community. Christians affect the world around them somewhat abstractly or disjointedly. They compete with sound bites over airwaves, withdraw into alternative schools, read only their own publications, and want the state to be run like a church. They invite their neighbors to a church experience but rarely to an interesting study of a film or an analysis of a politician's program. An exhibit in a museum is rarely studied with the thought in mind to compare it with what Christianity teaches about God, man, and life.

For many Christians there is almost no life of any kind outside their own fellowship and convictions. Their active world is limited to what is spoken about in church and what is found in so-called Christian bookstores, many of which carry only a small selection of books. As mentioned earlier, a regular bookstore will guide you to their various sections, such as Psychology, Travel, or Mysteries, a Christian bookstore needs to guide you to their book section because of the preponderance of various holy hardware—paintings, plaques, T-shirts, etc. Christians' concern often is protection from the temptation outside, and they escape into the inner sanctum. They are more interested in their personal happiness and how to have a personal relationship in a fragmented life than in what is real in God's creation. Whether God is really there, whether he is good and trustworthy, and how he is different from all the other gods on the marketplace of current religions is raising questions that they can only answer by affirming once again their personal faith. The Bible's "Thus says the Lord" of a more confident generation has become "This I affirm" in a time of religious and moral relativism.

When churches have such separated programs for their own adherents and identify themselves primarily by their denominational peculiarities, they take few serious stands that challenge the public. What makes them different from each other is more noticeable than what they actually believe and teach. They are not consulted as sources for information about how to understand life and its difficult problems from the answers of God's text but are rather known for their denominational particulars, their doctrines, and their more or less attractive programs for their own internal market of people. In this way they compete with their secular cousins such as country clubs, nature trails, concert halls, shopping malls, and other gatherings. They all offer similar ways to seek something spiritual in the midst of a world largely reduced to its material components.

We were in the final approach into a large airport from the north toward the eastern runway. We crossed suburbs with their lake access properties, their recreational fields and neat roads through newer developments, and their carefully divided plots. But now, the closer we came to landing, the emptier the land below us became. The private houses gave way to commercial usage, distribution centers with trailers backed against warehouse gates. No one would want to live this close to the noise of approaching aircraft.

A wide highway underneath passes between two enormous parking lots on either side of the road. To the west of the highway lies what must be a large shopping mall. A cluster of buildings in different shapes and sizes are glued together. The logo of this and that national brand store is recognizable from the air. The structure is surrounded by an almost circular parking lot with carefully drawn herringbone patterns of stripes in the pavement. Cars are assigned spaces close to entrances and under neatly spaced lights. It looks like a feeding trough for cattle or, in a more animated image from Texas farms farther away, like a sow nursing her many hungry piglets.

On the eastern side of the highway is another large building with a somewhat smaller parking area in the shape of a drive-in cinema lot. No cars are parked there. It is not a smaller mall, now discarded for lack of business and replaced by the larger one across the street. Instead the roof of the central building also has a logo that explains to the sky and anyone crossing it that this is a church building. Between airport and shopping mall, away from suburbia and its social castes, the logo announces that this is a church in much the same way a Ford dealer advertises cars, J.C. Penney its location as an anchor in a mall, or Hershey chocolate its product line.

This was a church. The sign let everyone know who or what they were and where they were located. But their fellowship was one that depended very much on advertised location, mobility of the members, and carefully announced programs to draw the customers.

The location placed the fellowship far away from where people lived, raised their children, and watered their lawns. For fellowship they depended on mobility by cars and on connectedness by wires. The programs to draw people there were themselves symbols of many of the things that describe the contemporary church. People gather at their leisure, when the church wins out in the competition for attention staged by a number of appealing alternatives. It becomes a chosen, convenient, and attractive activity. From that vantage point it is hard to realize that there is something perhaps somewhat incongruent about it all. A choice governed by convenience and pleasure leaves little room for the prophetic, social, and confrontational aspect of Christianity.

Amos went from his sheep and trees to the king's house and told the people of Israel what was wrong with them. Elijah spoke with Ahab to his face in the king's palace in the name of the God whom he served. Can the church still do that when it has made itself into such a separated, entertaining, and convenient commodity in the market? In such a fellowship the prophet is valued because he says what everyone wants him to say. Market forces, opinion polls, and management standards then become the criterion for a good shepherd.

We have shopping malls with all kinds of stores. They have become cities without inhabitants. Life there is made up of shoppers. They are fed in food courts not totally unlike farmyards with their mixture of smells. They are entertained in multi-screen movie theaters. It is all out there, more or less appealing to the tastes and budgets of visitors. You take what you want, and when you no longer like it, you can trade it in, up or down. At least one of the malls in America even makes weddings possible in a chapel right there among the other stores. Malls cater not only to the desire to find many choices at close proximity. They turn malling itself into an activity, where one often does not go with a distinct purpose or with a shopping list of necessary items, but where the activity itself becomes the occupation or business. Sales are frequently a side result of customers being drawn to things that more often awaken their dormant appetite than provide products or services that are really needed or wanted.

But people do not only go to the malls in order to shop for all kinds of things under one roof and within the reach of the parking lot. You also undoubtedly know friends who tell you, with some satisfaction and ingenuity in their voice, that they even do their exercises within the mall. Others go there from a desire to break out of their isolation and to meet people. It is relatively safe, air-conditioned, and colorful and presents a constantly changing scenery. Last week's "final sales" closed a store. New stores will come with opening bargains. The whole thing is rather entertaining and creates the impression of life on the move. You don't want to miss it!

Here then is life on both sides of the highway. Both offer their merchandise to the interested client. On the one side they suggest you try bathing suits or housewares or fashions before you surround yourself with cross-cultural smells in the food court. On the other side they may hand out gimmicks with "Try Jesus" or "Jesus is my copilot" as an invitation to follow up their pitches. They invite you to various groups of like-minded people, whether you are single or married, young or old, want to join or just visit to learn about relationships and prayer groups. Even discussions are often directed more at making you one of them than at helping you sort out what is true for anyone in a world full of beauty and contradictions, tricks, insecurities, and pain.

Churches often seem to compete, like malls, for the attention of people. That is probably not their intention, but the circumstances of our society produce that effect. They spend large sums and energy to be able to provide something for every taste, and it is on the level of taste that selections are made for one comfort zone or another. As the mall needs to attract a high turnover of the public to satisfy its stores, so the church presents an attractive facility with convenient parking as well as spiritual performances to increase the numbers, to fulfill its mission to the masses.

But in the evident parallel it is easily forgotten that church is not a function called to render a service, but a body of believers who primarily serve God and offer what is precious to him. They bring to God their attention, worship, joy and burdens, sorrow and grief. They admit that God is right about man, history, and life and death. They serve God and neighbor with what we all need to know and do, which quite often is something other than what we wish to do or would rather not know. People should come to church to learn from the Creator how to live in creation, not to dress their lonely lives with colorful activities or cook up better feelings.

Even with a genuine desire to alert others to this reality of God, man, and life, we can easily be distracted from the central affirmation of the Bible. There is a God, and he made us. We all need to know and acknowledge this. However, with the burden to tell it to our neighbors who are ignorant of God, we must not twist the example of St. Paul. His statement that he had "become all things to all people, that by all means I might save some" (1 Corinthians 9:22) can't be turned into a proposition that we become like others in all situations. Such adaptation leads to a dilution of content. When the messenger himself becomes the message, it will be impossible to convince anyone of what is important. St. Paul adapted his manner so that the content could be understood. He did not adapt the content so that his manner would be pleasing. Perhaps he would have stopped eating meat on occasions to talk to vegetarians. He would have learned local history to address a person from another country. He would have bowed in greeting rather than shake hands in order to do as the Thai do. But he never seemed to have stopped his direct, confrontational, and clearly-argued declaration of what is true in the real world to anyone under God and how we must respond in order to be truthful to it all.

Paul writes in 1 Corinthians 9:21 that to those outside the law he "became as one outside the law . . . that I might win those outside the law." To the Greeks Paul became like a Greek in order to tell them in their words and forms of communication that they must no longer be like Greeks in their beliefs, their practices, and their attitudes. He told them they had to turn "to serve the living and true God, and to wait for his Son from heaven, whom he raised from the dead, Jesus who delivers [them] from the wrath to come" (1 Thessalonians 1:9-10). Each idea in that sentence signifies the opposite of what the Greeks of Thessalonica had been taught all their lives. He also told them that they should not sleep around, but rather treat the body in a way that is holy and honorable. They should love their brothers, which I suppose, given the background of all of Scripture, is more than liking them, going fishing, and sharing the Word. They were to work honestly and win the respect of outsiders, far more than making a good living or being able to retire early to go on mission trips. And all of these subjects Paul talked about in the course of only two weeks before being thrown out of town (Acts 17:1-9).

Today we see things in "more sensitive" ways. We like to appear grand. We change the messenger and his podium into something that avoids such confrontation. We do not think people will like to come when their culture is not approved of. So we add Jesus to their areas of interest and blend him among their friends. We counsel them to seek a personal relationship with him. He will then become the family friend, doctor, spiritual advisor, and partner in prayer. But is this still the Jesus of history, the Christ on the cross, the blessing to many nations, and the Judge of the universe? The Bible announces his coming as a sacrifice and his coming again as the Judge of righteousness.

If church has been reduced to something similar to a shopping experience in the mall, can it still speak about life, God, and man in history? What does that similarity tell me about the moral and educational content I should study, learn, and accept before I can be discharged from home and school and church to actually live? Just as the tools given in school have often been dulled, the relationship with Jesus talked about in church does not alone give the content required to master life reasonably. The student and the Christian need more discernment than just good learning experiences and intentions. We need to know the world out there with all its wonder and all its pitfalls. We need to know what God had in mind when he made us and gave us dominion over creation, to work with our hands, and to distinguish between truth and falsehood, between good and bad government, between honest business practices and cheating the poor out of their coats, their wages, and their souls.

Doing the things I like and making choices largely along the lines of seeking fulfillment and pleasure has become a pattern in a culture that knows no other obligation than to satisfy personal needs and wants to feel good about itself as a human right. In the book *Shopping Mall High School*[7] the suggestion is made that the curriculum at many American schools now gives a similar experience to students and teachers as the malls do to us all. Students can study what they like, what they believe to be relevant to them personally. The focus is on personal interest, peer agreement, and enjoyable pursuits as an expression of personal development, growing self-esteem, and personal choice. Students do not primarily go to school because learning is a necessity and discovery is a benefit. They rarely see a link between learning the various skills of reading, writing, and arithmetic and the need for tools for critical thinking. Those skills are necessary to become aware of a real world. Yet what is in the real world is deemed less important than what the student wants to know about it for personal or political ends.

The curriculum today serves vastly reduced ends in relation to the objective world and largely broadened ends for personal development. It is based on the assumption that a self-confident person will later be able to manage life without all the detailed instruction about human beings, history, geography, and the world becoming accessible through foreign languages. Greater confidence in oneself, a more satisfied child, a motivated child are more important than a child who learns to recognize the perpetual human struggle or the more (and often less) human practices in various cultures and religions. Matters of the outside world, the lessons to be learned from history, the skills needed to tackle difficult tasks ahead are seen as of less importance than being able to feel good about oneself.

There is a thread through this that binds everything together in a similar approach to life's very different needs and experiences. The consumer in the mall, the student in the school, and the person with some spiritual desires or needs is able to achieve satisfaction because the standards are set by his personal needs and desires. He has become a god who fashions, to a very large extent, a world in his image. He is the self-confident manipulator and can be proud of his powers, until the choices and intentions of others crash upon him and reveal the futility of his earlier selfishness.

The consumer is encouraged to see only what he is looking for. He makes decisions on the basis of what he likes or finds personally fulfilling. He has little concern about what makes sense in the larger world of reality and has replaced it with a sensual gauge to tell him what feels good (cf. Ephesians 4:19). The desired end of feeling good, accepted, loved, and approved has determined the choice of panaceas. And often the church has become a participant in the vast experiment of how to satisfy the customer.

Both the mall with material goods on one side of the street and the hall with spiritual foods on the other keep their doors open and their parking lots ready to welcome clients with the selection of the day. The customer of the church also experiences all the attention, the attractive presentation in a safe and convenient location. He soon becomes convinced he needs what is offered but is not necessarily convicted of sin, righteousness, and judgment. For he is easily more attracted by the similarities of the places and the anticipated experiences than by the possible differences in content. He is in search of an experience, while the content of Christianity is more a message, leading to debate and comprehension. The knowledge of God starts with clear and intelligent discernment, not with a set of experiences. We have knowledge of God initially when we are convinced that he exists, that he is really there, as opposed to his nonexistence.

Knowledge of God continues with a discovery of who this God is, what he has said and done, why we should believe him or not, and how we should live as human beings. We come to know the truth by way of clear distinctions among the alternatives set before us by life, philosophy, or our neighbors.

This road of discovery from facts to knowledge and wisdom is increasingly bypassed, for it requires a certain effort, steady interest, and a careful selection according to criteria of truth, which need to be reasonably established and weighed. Such effort is countered by the easy and almost effortless access to sensual experiences, by shopping for alternatives in a world that has replaced sensitivity with sensuality. There has been a marked shift in the way content reaches our mind. God's Word is verbal and sequential communication to our minds, where it has to make sense in order to be reasonably understood. In the past merchants advertised their goods by announcing what was available (the old meaning of the word *advertisement*). But now, and parallel to the greater use of visual and sound images to create or awaken dormant appetites, the church often feels obliged to use sensual means to appeal. Easily overlooked is the resulting appetite for more of what can only dilute the comprehension of God's Word. We have become a generation demanding signs and wonders from the church, for the message of God, creation, the Fall, and redemption is no longer sufficiently beautiful.

Many in the church are aware of the effect of this change in our way of understanding Christianity. Advertisement with a focus on the fun and entertainment of having more things creates needs and appetites and helps define expectations and priorities. Questions of quality, truth, and objective need are easily pushed aside, for they require time, distance, and reflection. It is easier not to raise them. But we must be careful—we now know that they may even be eliminated, not only by cultural and moral factors, but by the human brain that never developed enough to raise them in the first place. Jane Healey and Neil Postman show the effect of heightened visual, in contrast to verbal, stimulation on the developing brain. They point out how the actual physical development in the brain is to a surprising degree directed by external stimuli. Failing to develop all the areas that govern rational thought leads to much greater difficulty later, when the person needs to use critical differentiation, but the tools for that have not been developed.

Visual input is observed uncritically as a whole and immediate impression. It requires little critical understanding. It is like a visit to a theme park with fast-moving, colorful, extraordinarily stimulating impressions that follow each other in rapid succession. By contrast verbal input needs to be understood to make an impression. A sentence has to be heard in a linear fashion—the subject generally precedes the verb and object. "Who says what to whom?" needs to be recognized before the content can sink in and be remembered. The young brain is stimulated by conversation and language to grow such abilities of understanding and discernment, so that the mind is then engaged as an analyst, not a receptacle. It is stimulated to compare, to remember, and to use imagination.

Real physical damage is done to our view of things, our range of expectations and field of interest, when most of our information comes as sensual stimuli without passing through the selective grid of the brain. Little wonder then that much of ordinary life can no longer interest or occupy children, who from an early age are used to exaggerated colors, sizes, and events. Without deliberate and prolonged training in the use of the mind, which begins with reading and being read to and continues into the pleasures of lengthy discussions and detailed research, it hardly surprises us that conversation among adults rarely goes beyond a sensual experience of one sports team beating the other or one stock climbing faster than another. The most interesting things of life are now the most entertaining, the most active, the most sensually stimulating. Intellectual and moral discussion has far fewer participants, but the consequences of this shift away from the intellect are drastic in the lives of everyone.

Perhaps that is the reason for my surprise at the direction that much of Christianity has taken in both content and methods. Instead of competing for the minds and hearts of people, the process itself, including the setting of the church plant, the program, and the performance, appeals to the visual, sensual, and emotional sides of people. Their response is more controlled by what they see than by what they hear, unless they can at least visualize what they hear in personal testimonies, human-interest stories, and the quasi-equivalent of crime reporting on TV, in the form of personal confessions.

Instead of maintaining a prophetic and priestly office of the church in public, "church" has become for many one more location for a performance of a different kind. What is put into the show competes on the wider market for attention. The content, the declaration, is diluted by adjustments to match what works in the market. The product is adjusted to buyers' tastes. The profit numbers depend on what you can sell and how much the client thinks he needs it now.

Marketing skills, advertising, colorful packaging, and much talk stimulate need and can then easily make up for what is lacking in the quality of the merchandise, the substance of a subject in school, or the truthfulness and solidity of Christianity. The quantity of buyers, the turnover, and the growth pattern in the church easily replace the need to insist on quality. Profit speaks, while the prophet is silenced. In our modern market context with its mentality, people will have a hard time distinguishing between an anointing with snake oil and one with the Holy Spirit of God. They have a desire to have religion, but not necessarily according to the truth. They seek the approval of their friend Jesus in some personal relationship, but they rarely know the Lord, whose Word guides us through the real world of nastiness, doubts, and suffering.

We must not quickly conclude that these concerns merely push us back to what is old-fashioned, traditional, or common. The Holy Spirit is not old-fashioned. Paul sought to speak to people in all kinds of settings, from riverbanks to synagogues and lecture halls, to the prisoners and guards around him. Paul exhibited much "modern" flexibility in form, but never in content.

We should consider how much the setting, the building, the mannerisms can support or distract from or even dilute the message. The packaging of the teaching of the Bible in music, fine clothes, and spiritual language cloaks the truth, making it easier or more difficult to hear and understand it as the truth of God and man, of life, death, and redemption.

My view from the airplane placed the church building somewhat symmetrically on the other side of the street from the shopping mall. Both had a similar approach and external appearance. You go to either place to get what you want to find, in a context you prefer. You make your choice to meet your personal needs. The visit to either parking lot is an event, something to do, an experience that meets a personal need. And you can leave when you want to. And you never have to go that road again.

But that church with its presence outside of town is only then a constant reminder of life, with its questions and doubts, when the content of what is declared and demonstrated there is solid, reasonable, provocative, and comforting. It should want to be a place where people are presented with the answers God gives in his letters to man, a teaching of a certain content and a view of truth to prick their consciences, to challenge their own thinking, and to critique their private conclusions.

It should be sensitive to the fact that its very location does not reinforce such content, even if it is given. The church is removed from the core of larger life and has become a feedlot like so many others in the Texas landscape and satisfies personal needs. When those are no longer met, one can always cross the street and try someplace else, making the rounds in another mall.

Many argue that the church needs to attract modern people with newer methods to hear the truth of Christ. We know that many have been turned off from earlier situations of organized religion in buildings to which one has little personal relationship and where parking is always a problem. We also know that overly stimulated people, immersed almost constantly in sound and sight experiences, need to be stimulated again to even give the message a hearing. In our democratic experience, in a world with so many private and public opinions, we accept that many people don't want to become subject to any authority other than the one they like and find appealing. They find their own personal way and want to be accepted for their personal testimony, express their personal taste, and make their personal experiences and purchasing decisions.

Such interest runs in line with pragmatism everywhere. We want an explanation of how things work and then repeat whatever works. Likewise we think practical consequences of faith in Christ will appeal to people. It will attract and convince people directly. But such pragmatism may turn into a habit of neglecting the intellectual in favor of the experiential, of denigrating thought and comparison and instead valuing testimonies of personally enriching experiences.

It has often been pointed out that the modern world with its possibilities exposes us to alternatives, breaking up traditions and developing curiosity. This is a practical result of democracy, of the priesthood of all believers, of the self-made man on the basis of merit rather than class. But there is a negative aspect to this as well. For the many possibilities have also made it so much more difficult to decide finally for any one thing with any serious commitment. That is so in relationship to one wife, loyalty on the job, a place to put down roots and to stand for God rather than gods. Given the multitude of things offered, it becomes very implausible to us that anything is really true, good, and right. So much the master of their own dreams and opportunities, it is difficult for people to wake up to the reality of God, to a defined creation, and an absolute right and wrong.

So perhaps the packaging of the gospel in too many techniques, too many distractions, too much color, music, and games makes that gospel in the end more implausible for our contemporary world. When the news about God and Christ is wrapped into personal stories, the experience of relationships, the pleasant company of like-situated people for the growth of the membership lists, does the good news even get a hearing? When does the proclamation become so adjusted to the audience's self-defined needs that the content is lost altogether?

The rise of focus groups, house churches, weekly revivals, and independent neighborhood churches gives every sign of growth and interest in Christianity. But together with it can also rise a degree of doubt in the certainty of objective truth. No other than C. S. Lewis wondered how much the spread of denominations undermines in a subtle way the very concept of truth. Perhaps there has been too much attention paid to the needs largely perceived by each participant or member and not enough to those addressed by God to the whole human race. There may be much sorrow, sin, and spiritual desire, but these are only valuable when they lead to repentance.

An advertisement in a Christian paper in New York recently invited people to a fellowship where "Faith in Christ" was set as "the only confession required." That should strike us all as odd, since an earlier church made every effort to define very carefully the Apostolic Confession about the three persons of the Holy Trinity.

The danger is that when we try too hard to adjust the message to the stated needs of the audience, the real message of God becomes more and more implausible to them. In their sense of freedom and self they determine what they want, need, and believe. People used to do that often with objects. The Israelites did it with a golden calf, which they called their god who had brought them out of Egypt. They had a faith, constituted a loving community, and gave their personal testimony and funds. But they were terribly wrong, since a piece of gold jewelry crafted from their offerings no God does make.

Catering to the market criteria of successful strategies, growing numbers, and a favorable response, the church is widely in danger of bowing to idols of its own making. I have been with missionaries in Russia who "came to share their relationship with Jesus." I find no record of the apostles doing that anywhere in the Roman world or the early church. They spoke of God, truth, righteousness, and repentance. Numbers alone in Bible studies or in attendance at church, the frequency of conversions, statistics of those who responded to invitations give scant evidence of a change of thought, purpose, social responsibilities, goals in life, or even the level of debate in public about the basis for a moral society.

It is good to offer to bury people with any faith and any budget, even from a commercial interest. By the time a person has died, that is an act of kindness, grace, and compassion with a business angle. However, what is set out as Christianity in our day has often very little to do with the Bible or the historic continuity of Christian teaching about how to view the world, to be in it but not of it, or the Jesus of history. He has long been buried, hidden in every "faith" that is in search of meeting any budget.

6

THE CHURCH OF
ST. BARNUM

It has been said that you can sell a guy anything if you only market it right.

Robert de Niro plays a protective and skeptical and obnoxious father in the film *Meet the Parents*. He is a former CIA agent and is determined to protect his daughter, and himself. The meeting with the new boyfriend of his beautiful daughter is a terrible experience for everyone. At every turn he gives the young man a hard time. He critiques him, lays traps, mocks him, and embarrasses him on every occasion. In addition to all the boyfriend's sweat and worry over how to respond to this possessive father and how to repair the damage incurred from putting his foot into his mouth so many times, there is the discovery of a former boyfriend during this dramatic weekend. While the current one may be more interesting and creative, the former one has recently made money on the stock market. He is building himself a new home, obviously without much taste, that is too large but a good thing to show what money can buy. When asked why he salvaged wood from an old Nantucket church for his specious modern house, he states that he is a Christian who wanted to go all the way and follow Jesus even in his carpentry profession. That relationship to Jesus also gets mentioned when, finding out that the guest is a Jew, the old boyfriend pauses briefly and then covers his surprise with, "Ah, so was Jesus."

The film's caricature makes the Christian quite deliberately a careless, superficial, but materially successful show-off, a somewhat sleazy character. The reference to Jesus does not hide but accentuates his obnoxious character. It is embarrassing to parade around with "my" Jesus when there is no reason for it. Most of the time it is merely a way to support or cover up a fundamental personal vanity. All it accomplishes is to justify a life, belief, and actions in public without any explanations apart from a personal faith. A relationship to Jesus does not make up for any lack of moral character or genuine wisdom and sensitivity. The young man here is obnoxious, insensitive, uncultured, and arrogantly self-righteous. He connects his money, success, manners, and performance to his faith and thereby justifies it. He does not have to explain, he has no doubts, and he is not part of a larger human community. He is merely right with everything—his Jesus, his money, and his decisions. That all shows the extreme lightness of his faith and gives good opportunities to anyone wishing to rob Christianity of much of its credibility.

When Christians are often seen in this way today, it is in part due to the deliberate rejection of Christianity by a secular world that wishes to reduce all of life to the flat dimension of what works pragmatically in the real world. Technocrats of any shade have little interests in the life of the mind, in value differentiation and the moral and philosophical questions of what ought or ought not to be done. They manage well what is and can be but have no measure to know what should or should not be.

However, Christians themselves often also bring this rejection upon themselves. When we abandon the larger content of the Bible, which addresses all of life, and reduce its importance to personal edification, spirituality, and private interpretation, we also become less knowledgeable, less interested in truth. We withdraw into personal camps with tightly held private opinions and are satisfied to remain in ignorance about the world around us. All our interest is then focused on "now," "us," and "peace." Rather than believing in "the light of the world" or "the bread of life," we have reduced Christianity to personal salvation, without being aware of the problems this creates. We reflect more on what God has done in the limited sphere of our personal life than on what he has done in history at large, which of course also affects our lives.

This shift from public and historical declaration to private and existential opinion has contributed to a loss of perspective inside the church. Simultaneously it has contributed to a loss of credibility and significance of the church to the outside world. The enormous impact and transforming power of the Bible in the history of our culture, where it had a powerful and culture-changing influence in economic, artistic, scientific, and social development, is understood to be a thing only of the past. The weight of its message is minimized in any public sense. What remains is that individuals go through a personal conversion and affiliate with a church community as a matter of taste, preference, and a sense of belonging. From here on out they join everyone else and talk about "values" instead of what is true, factual, and coherent.

The real weight of Christianity has to be established again and then be carried in each generation by contributions from Christians in all spheres of life. This requires that work, argumentation, passion, and intellectual answers relate to the coherence and beauty of the biblical view of the real world, where the truth is established and can stand up under critical eyes. We largely fail to demonstrate such a connection between thought and practice, between ideas and efforts, between the teaching of the Bible concerning life and the change of human thought and action as a result of it. Our concerns as Christians no longer measure up to the big questions of God and truth, of reason and folly. Instead much of the church is satisfied to shrink its proclamation to match personal interests, provide personal peace, and nurture good feelings.

The response from those outside is at best tolerance, at worst indifference or hostility. Nothing really stirs up their curiosity if the church herself has little more to offer than a spiritual pacifier to still a crying baby, hold the hand of the lonely, and provide a safe environment for the unstable and a belief in personal salvation.

Much ignorance about the truth of Christianity comes from a lack of historical overview. As a culture we look ahead, are optimistic, and live by hope without reference to what the Bible describes as weights from the past. We always feel we should forget about the past and avoid its consequences. Sometimes the need to create distance from what happened before comes from a sense of resentment. It is then an almost adolescent-like reaction to the authority of truth, the limitations of reality, and God's definitions. Resentment, like a filter, often rejects biblical Christianity on the basis of some poor earlier impressions about what is assumed to be Christian. Happily there is often more to the life of the church than what is noticed by her critics.

Yet much of the church has reduced the weight of God's Word and truth in history to an extreme lightness of faith. The Bible and the church should provide provocative, powerful, and challenging confrontations with intellectual reasoning and practical compassion. A healthy word and a healthy community of people marked the work of believers in earlier generations.

In the course of a very few decades much of the church has embraced the way of mass culture in its drive to reduce everything to play and attractive entertainment. It has bowed to the demands of a consumer society and offers a message that more often distracts for the moment than comforts for the long run. Adjustments in content and form to match the perceived needs of future possible converts eat away at the content necessary to understand God, the fall of man, and redemption. Marketing priorities preside. The product is matched to the customer's expectations. There is little room for the doctor to prescribe the medicine or for God to set forth judgment and conditions for redemption. Both sources could give much deeper insight if it only mattered at all to the patient.

Instead the church has adapted its soul and life and teaching to appeal to modern man, whose whole perception has been altered by a culture that allows him to expect entertainment, fun, and easy success. The believer-to-be expects to be confirmed in views already held, whether they are of his assumed greatness or his experienced inferiority. He is promised his own personal relationship with Jesus and is sent out to make his own experiences. He will believe whatever seems to him most plausible without any real outside controlling references in reason, church, or Scripture, for to them he will give his own interpretation as well. The only important date and event in history is "the day I met Jesus" or "the day I took Jesus into my heart." To the host of other experiences he now adds also his conversion and repentance as experiences without much content or without much awareness of the consequences.

Dare I suggest that there is perhaps a parallel to the expressed need of some women to have a pregnancy experience before they get to be too old to have a baby? It is the experience as an experience that matters more than any understanding of the larger picture—the looming consequences, the child's needs for years ahead, and the changed life for the whole family. We live in a world where all events have meaning and where one can't ever escape the consequences.

Hardly any reference to outside factors checks the holy texts believers cite or the spiritual experience they relate. Their self-esteem has grown marvelously, but the needed discernment, wisdom, and courage is sorely lacking. They have a personal relationship with a deity, a text to give them authority, a way to approve all things as the will of God for their lives. They also have an excuse not to feel responsible for the rest of the world: *All people need to do for similar happiness is to believe as I do. Were they to come to this, they would share my experiences of the wonderful things God has planned for them as well.*

Adherents to Eastern and other exotic religions tend to be admired for their devotion, their intellectual sacrifice, and their submission to spiritual disciplines. Christians were in the past noticed for the opposite—their coherent arguments, intellectual rigor, practical works of kindness, reliability, generosity, and hard work. This attitude toward all of life flowed from the mandate to subdue the earth and to have dominion.

These were results of a biblical view of things. They were like plants that grew from the seed thrown on good soil, which was watered, did not fall on rocky ground, and took deep root to live even under the heat of a summer's day. There are real and practical consequences to people believing certain things from their biblical worldview. One can't explain the humanitarian, social, and scientific efforts in our culture except on the background of the Bible's teaching. Like yeast the results gradually spread through the whole loaf of the human reality and produced intellectual, moral, and individual conversions. Even today, several generations removed from a widespread acceptance of this teaching, the memory lingers, and the fruit is still visible. It is so outstanding that in a crisis any concerned Buddhist, Muslim, or materialist will seek shelter, health, and education in our countries rather than in their own cultures.

Without such visible fruits we are prone to be noticed only as one more religious group with its internal convictions. Love, community, and kindness speak out loudly. But they should be framed by hard work, intelligence, moral rigor, professionalism, and entrepreneurial engagement as a part of compassion. Sharing one's time and food is no more spiritual than, for instance, creating jobs and seeking justice through better laws.

Without these latter goals we will present few challenges to the outside world. Democratic pluralism and personal rights are wonderful accomplishments and express the importance of valuing people as persons. But they have lately contributed to the loss of the concept and meaning of "true truth." For they can't be beneficial when they are separated from the Bible, which gave birth and definition to them in the first place. Tragically much Christian teaching leaves people only with the private side of faith. It fails to stress the relationship also to a "public" truth for all persons anywhere.

Students at a Christian college outside New York City were readily appreciated for their honesty, simplicity, and single purpose. They would make good baby-sitters and honest checkout clerks. However, they were rarely known for being better informed, more serious, interesting, knowledgeable, or intellectually challenging than students from other colleges. Their ethics were appreciated and stood out in a time of college brawls and easy sexuality. But their minds, their curiosity, their field of study and anticipated occupation were not part of what they communicated to their employers or the community at large. It did not help, of course, that the school itself offered no classes to the general public to introduce the relevance and truthfulness of a Christian view to the community—for instance, on economics, psychology, or art.

From outside the church Christians often appear somewhat simplistic. A good effort has been made in more recent years to counter this through better schools, social programs in the city, and wider political involvement. Yet many perceive Christians as quite superficial, self-righteous, and overconfident because God has already forgiven them. Such believers seem little concerned about what the light and truth are, which their forefathers carried with effort to the wider world. Because they are right with God, they are ready to believe that they are right about everything. This inevitably contributes to a reaction and even an aversion to Christians in our pluralistic culture, in which anyone having a firm opinion in any but private areas is suspect. Yet Christians defend their view with reference to their personal God, but rarely with any reference to an objective creation.

Perhaps they assume that the grace of God gives them superior qualities. I frequently found that students with "Jesus in their heart" had little interest in questions about normal life and little curiosity to help them grow in wisdom, knowledge, and perspective. They found no pleasure in knowing more of the human reality or anything factual about the world around them. People as persons did not really interest them. They applied labels to them like redeemed and unredeemed, Christian and non-Christian. That was sufficient to catalog all reality in a very simplistic way. No amount of trouble in the world around us, no intellectual challenge about good and evil, no high or low point of history, no sincere appreciation of what human beings do with their minds and hands even when they are not believers could come close to them and challenge their perception, their faith, their life, or their concerns. They felt secure and knew no fear and trembling, perhaps mainly because they knew so little about anything.

This perception of Christians as a peculiar group of people with their own cultural and social patterns has a safe place in the pluralistic landscape. Pluralism affirms the distinctions that Christians rightly insist on. There is a problem, however, when Christians see themselves as better per se and thus justified in the way they live, often in isolation from others around them. They admit no critique from the outside. They are what they are by the grace of God. Insidiously, such grace encourages a high view of oneself, for one easily forgets the common brokenness that makes grace so necessary.

Grace is an indication of our flaws, not of our superiority. Grace is certainly not a rag to cover up limitations of knowledge and a lack of wisdom about large areas of life and the world around us. Grace does not cover ignorance but guilt. While Christians should believe that God will in the future separate the wheat from the tares, many seem to assume that grace already gives them the right and mandate to impose themselves as if they were already perfect. They judge, reject, and condemn what does not fit into their particular mold or expectations. They create their kingdom now, immanently and present.

They also set themselves apart by a tribal vocabulary or by holding certain political and social positions without rhyme or much reason. The group is boxed in, becomes narrow and unapproachable, and quickly receives a label. By their language and their withdrawal from the public market of ideas, they create a ghetto. They feel safe there; they like it. Their faith is their fortress, and they have little interaction with the rest of the world, creation, or life in the market. They rarely carry the truth to the public square. Their testimony is mostly to themselves as a distinct group. They justify this with submission to God and avoidance of any relation to the real world, which the God of the Bible created. Outsiders are expected to take an existential leap into their fold. On the surface they believe themselves to be right, to have greater peace and more joy than other groups. Beneath lies often a world of fear, anger, and avoidance, for their faith is not the result of a desire to understand the truth of God and human historic reality. It has rarely been toughened in the fire of doubt and adversity. Their armor is not so much the buckle of truth, the breastplate of righteousness, and the shield of faith, but a community of words with a mystic spirituality and a sword of anger.

Pagan cultures were changed and people were converted when Jews and Christians ventured out from behind the ghetto walls to address human need with the power of God's Word, the Bible, and not only with words of condemnation. The text, given by the only God whose existence alone explains our existence, speaks to everyone, not only to the faithful. In the past that Word broke down doors, disarmed arguments, brought light into darkness, and sent people across the world to shout it into the lives of grieving humanity. That Word of substance called for engagement, not denial and withdrawal. It had a certain content, which gave rise to a powerful life of the mind, to creative intervention in human suffering, as well as to ennobling work and artistic variety.

There is a second reason for the absence of the Bible in the market. The community wants to be entertained, not enlightened. In response we have silenced the clear ring of the Word by cracking the bell. The Word as a complex and unified statement is torn apart by selectively choosing texts that are personally meaningful, relevant, and memorable without regard for their context, their meaning in the flow of revelation. Favorite texts express the readers', not the author's, preference. They are used to meet the average needs of peers in focus groups and home gatherings. Once the teaching of the Bible gave power to resist injustice, death, and oblivion. Pluralism, democratic variety, and personal faiths have replaced an accessible truth once woven into a fabric of reality. The world is now viewed through glasses of personal preference. The Bible is to people no longer that set of lenses through which what is real and what we need to know about it are brought together to help us live truthfully as members of the human race since Adam.

Biblical Christianity speaks of fundamental building blocks that, once in place and arranged in order, make human life possible. These are specific interlocking realities without which the terms *biblical* and *Christianity* no longer mean anything. The Bible does not give us verses like souvenirs from different trips. We have a text that describes a view of the whole world. All the pieces hang together; each of them sheds light on the others. The meaning gets clearer as more pieces are brought together to construct the whole. The text is like letters that inform us about the bigger picture of the world we live in. They address diverse situations in many different forms. But together the text explains to us the world we inhabit.

A few of these building blocks should be mentioned. Without any one of them the whole structure collapses. The foundation is that life for a human being is only possible with the eternal existence of the person of God. He thinks, feels, and acts in time. He made us in his image, unlike all else around us, which follows only programs and instincts. We are in part tied to the closed system of nature but also express real freedom and responsibility, without which there would be no literature, no law, and no love.

The Bible then speaks of the tragic fall of man to explain how God can be good though we see wrong and death all around us. It continues with the promise of salvation to come through the death of Christ, the Judge of the universe, the one who resolves our legal problem of guilt and, through his resurrection, the problem of how to be free from death and causes us to live again in a restored creation.

In the Bible we read of the historic events of the birth of Jesus through the Virgin Mary with its reasonable explanation. There are no freak miracles, no unexamined events. People who are more interested in facts than faith describe a physical resurrection of that same Jesus in time and space. He has promised to return to earth in the future to demolish evil and death itself by bringing justice, peace, and restoration in real history, starting with Jerusalem.

All these are building blocks to form a structure of coherent thought and historic reality without which you do not have what makes up a Christian understanding of reality and history.

In the same reality we note that there is no human life unless it is a fact described by certain components, such as physical life and individuality. These components demand respect for the "inalienable rights" from "their Creator": the freedom of ideas, movement, association, and creativity as well as physical and legal protection from conception on. Our system of laws, our description of life in literature and the arts, any of our languages and patterns of trade and relationships bear witness to this view of the definite distinctive of human life. Animals make sounds, mate, and have a dread of danger. But there is no evidence that these reactions are the same as active speech, love, and fear of annihilation or death. For their sounds are not used to lie, their tools are never improved upon, and they don't worry about ecology.

We do well to remember how much the teaching of the Bible through the centuries laid our Western cultural roots and many of its realities about individuals and society, about work and government, about law and freedom. That bell loudly rang with more than music. The spoken word in response to the text of the Bible demanded and created the challenged and creative mind, without which human awakening to moral courage, intellectual responsibility, and artistic endeavors are always opposed or even suppressed. Yet the culture nurtured from such parents is increasingly no longer borne up by what "church" as an event has turned into under the effect of competing noises in more recent times.

At one time the Christian church gave the tone, made the music, and produced the harmonies of life. It was directed by a vision of the wholeness of life, in which each part had a proper place. Of course, this did not proceed from the hands of men and women without including at times great injustice, flawed efforts, and wicked deceptions. In the name of God people sought their own triumph, personal advantage, and unbridled exploitation of others in the world around them. They often pursued their kingdom rather than God's, from Charlemagne to Napoleon to Hitler to Stalin.

The same Bible also gave a set of references against which all human action could and should be judged. Prophets, kings, and common people, even the chosen people of Israel, were many times exposed as sinners. Both the book of God's Word (the Bible) and the book of God's work (the reality of creation) were measures. Both standards, mutually supporting one another, could be used to raise the call for justice and rationality in the midst of human folly and sin. Both standards existed outside the human imagination and will. They gave a mandate to use human freedom for what one wanted to do in the limits of what one ought to do. Capability was encouraged within the boundaries of moral accountability. There was freedom and creativity within the form of an already existing real world.

The reduction of Christian content to personal and more emotional concerns is a great tragedy when seen against the greater flow of the power of the Bible to transform ideas and practices over generations. The horizon against which things were measured and considered has fallen to the ceiling of our own perception, selfish wants, and personal rights. Rationality has been sacrificed on the altar that celebrates selfish interests and personal views like adolescent tantrums. It may happen quite innocently and without malice, simply from a lack of interest or burden. Yet soon such a personal view of rights has little to do with the liberties and rights extruded from the Bible and protected under the U.S. Constitution. The new view reveals more of the constitutional makeup of the modern citizen, who abandons the rights once granted by the Sovereign God and replaces them with the rights and claims of the sovereign individual.

It is doubly tragic and must involve shameful decisions when this denial of the Word and work of God is encouraged by the church. A continuous interest in truth should stir her to know what is true and just to her Lord. The church has a priestly and prophetic calling from her Lord. Both Word and creation should inform her perspective and hope. But the neglect of one will fail the other, and the church will minister to perceived, not real, needs.

In recent generations portions of the church abandoned God, first, by suggesting that the Bible is full of error. This left us with merely another human document of religious interest. Believers did this under the influence of rationalist thinking over the past two hundred years. The church became the arbiter of the text, determining what God could and could not do. Then the theological streams of the Death of God movement in the U.S. and The Gospel of Christian Atheism in Europe suggested there was enough evidence to conclude that God did not exist or that he had in fact died. The experience of horror and inhumanity in the twentieth century without any evident intervention from God gave rise to this existentialist view. The earlier rejection, on philosophical grounds, of the Bible as truthful and reliable had dug this black pit for theology in the first place. For without a historically truthful text there is no way to understand the fall of man and the subsequent abnormality and tension in history of a good God and a world of evil. Without the Bible there is no way to separate God from the evil events in history or even to conclude that anything is abnormal in the first place. Where there is no *norm* outside of history, history itself is merely *normal*.

The more recent form of destroying the Creator's information is to select, without much regard for the context, Bible verses for any occasion, depending on personal needs and interests. You take what you want and what you feel you need. This is the existentialist method of making your own selections at will, using the Bible only as a quarry for that purpose. When you feel lonely or overwhelmed, guilty or in need of a moral boost, church will give you the kick you need. When you experience stress or boredom, the need for community and the comfort of others, the church will have the right group, offer therapy, guide you to their book table, and describe a model for you to associate with. The church will offer entertaining performances, well-managed group dynamics, and a safe fellowship of equals for a generation that expects simple, quick, and pleasing solutions, because in every other area we have also been spoiled by ready access to entertainment. The craving for fast-action stimuli, loud colors, and constantly changing scenery will be met with programs that focus on approval, satisfaction, and affirmation.

St. Paul faced similar attitudes on his travels in the Roman Empire. He contrasts the outlook of Rome and Athens with the understanding of Christians and warns believers to stay away from the sensual pursuits of pagans. "Sensuality" in Ephesians 4:17-19 refers to physical and material experiences without careful moral or philosophical determination. Without a well-trained critical mind and an educated conscience, our senses respond to stimulated appetites and leave out the mind's moral evaluation. We have senses with which to recognize and enjoy material things in a real creation. But without intellectual reflection the sensual relates more to the physical in us, seeking only felt, or sensual, satisfaction. Without the additional moral dimension of what ought or ought not to be, mere sensuality often leads to impurity through cupidity. Paul admonishes us to seek control over sensuality through sensitivity to moral and ethical considerations. Without it our minds are empty and our effort to live lacks a moral compass. Sensuality will not stimulate or satisfy the moral/cultural side of human existence.

Paul contrasts sensuality with the need to be sensible, sensitive, and intelligent. When he speaks in other places of crucifying the flesh, he does not advocate the denial of a material life, real pleasures, or the meeting of material needs. *The flesh* is a term describing a horizontal focus on things, tastes, and instincts that can easily be satisfied without any regard or respect for moral/cultural considerations as intelligent beings. There is no place for asceticism in the Bible. Spirituality has nothing to do with becoming independent of a real body, real food, and real work. Even the call to fast is a call to focus at times on things other than a schedule of meals and occupations. It is not an initiation to otherness, transcendence, or indifference to the created world of space and time, of food and bodies, of work and love.

Our interest should include life in all its parts and complexity, not merely material and other sensual possibilities and desires. In the created world each fact also has a dimension of purpose that the Creator had in mind. Each choice requires a moral consideration as well as a factual one. There is nothing neutral in a created world. All that exists is there because of someone's choice, effort, and determination, whether God's or man's. As choice-makers all human beings are not only faced with a world of what *is* and its real possibilities—they also stand under an obligation to recognize moral restraints as well as mandates to act in line with what *ought* to be.

The church must speak of this double framework of being and morals, of what is and what ought to be. Yet often she is today torn into either the extreme of always moralizing along narrow criteria of obedience as a sign of spirituality and withdrawal from fact and reason or of copying secular ways and appeals to satisfy the sensual needs of people with a musical band, the total show, the choreography on stage, the offerings of the marketplace, the physical workout, or the emotions and the fellowship of satisfied customers. Believers justify the latter easily in the language of spiritual needs and blessings; yet their model comes more from Sesame Street and Disney than from the life of people born to create an intelligent, loving, and creative/artistic community of God's people. We should ask how much the existence and appeal of theme parks in our culture has led to people's expecting the church to supply a theme experience. Is it still possible to speak of the things of truth, reality, and the intellect in a culture so attuned to sensual satisfaction? How much does the longing for a good and entertaining time make it impossible to give God's sharp and piercing truth even a hearing?

In part this is the dilemma of the postmodern mind. We admit readily that we always see things from the angle of an individual subject. Postmodernism, however, leaves one with that as the only point of light, because it denies that anything can be known of an objective world. Even the Creator can't tell us things from his objective perspective. Reality itself can't be expressed as existing outside our perception of it. Therefore today alone matters, as if it stands by itself without any awareness of the continuity of history. Only the present stimulates, defines, and matters, it is claimed. Certainty exists by means of a personal and sensual experience. Such experience makes you feel good, even when there is no confidence that anything *is* true or good. From childhood on in schools, church, and media, very limited knowledge of the world, history, and a general purposeful pattern of life is given. An optimistic and affirmative agenda always satisfies, pleases the eye, and tickles the ear with no criteria to evaluate experiences on the basis of benefit or harm in the long run. With the focus on just today, the world tomorrow will have to provide for itself.

We have arrived where we are because of a slide from an initial rejection of the Creator God of the Bible to an uncertainty and indeterminacy about nature, man, meaning, and morals. With God largely shoved into the private sphere, there is nothing that can be said about the image of God either, nor about purpose, morals, and meaning in any public sense.

The church does not often enough stand against this mind-set. Instead she nurtures it with an overemphasis on the subjective. Insidiously she removes any truly objective reference point when the individual speaks of his or her personal God, Lord, Savior, friend.

What was traditionally "the whole counsel of God" (Acts 20:27)—i.e., the declaration of the Creator about his being, purposes, and judgment—is now replaced by a private counseling experience, shared personal testimony, group therapy, and repeated personal affirmations. Reality has been shrunk from substantial certainty about a real world open for discovery to subjective, relational certitude about personal opinions, preferences, and therapeutic needs. The objective has slipped away and been replaced by the subjective. The world out there no longer exists with any importance. The inner perspective matters more and is very similar to the personal vision of things. It becomes a virtual reality of one's own making. Who cannot relate to that?

In history the impact of Jewish and Christian teaching swept over Europe through the centuries with much effect in moral, cultural, and practical matters because it exposed and clarified the hideous inhumanity, insufficiency, and irrationality of pagan religions from the Germanic tribes back to Greece and Rome. It made a solid case against which even Islam later could not win. It taught and lived in some substantial, though often poor, way a whole worldview, not just a personally relevant faith. It argued its case against traditions, personal sensibilities, and fate. It proclaimed the truth of heaven in the midst of the valleys of human thought. Christianity did not focus on Rome, Constantinople, Wittenberg, or California, but on God's historical work in and around Jerusalem.

St. Paul and others brought this perspective to Europe and into the Greek and Roman world. Paul changed the worldview of the young believers in Thessalonica in two weeks. He did not decorate or embellish their religion but placed the intellectual ax at the root of their thinking. Consequently they understood a needed change in their thought and practice: The biblical view produced radical ("at the roots") change in all areas of life, not just a pluralistic variant. He did this with much psychological sensitivity, for he knew how hard it is for people to turn their whole worldview upside down. He cared for them with gentleness, like a mother (1 Thessalonians 2:7) and worked side by side with them like a brother, not wanting to be a burden to them (v. 9). He encouraged, comforted, and urged each of them like a father (v. 11). Yet what changed their view so profoundly was less the fact that Paul loved them than that he spoke not as another wise man, but rather gave them the Word of God, a text leading to the discovery of reality in its truth content and historic relevance (v. 13).

The believers in Thessalonica left their many gods of the Greek countryside for the one God of heaven. Only God could be the foundation of anything claiming to be true, original, and sovereign, without confusion or competition from other deities tied to changing seasons, powers, and events. The Thessalonians abandoned unpredictable fates for the living God. Their immoral deities were really more like naughty men who were merely bigger than mortals. The moral God of the Bible now replaced them. The Greek view of a cyclical nature of history was abandoned for a linear view, where purpose, progress, and an aim for all effort existed from the beginning. Resignation under the fates was rejected, for they do not allow an awareness of moral and factual responsibility. History made sense now, a real and open road to be carved out of the mountains ahead. Whatever was done would be judged in a moral universe. For guilt and judgment, there was a way to escape the coming wrath through belief in God's forgiveness through Christ's work. Finally, all this was part of a purposeful human existence that would continue after death, since God had raised Jesus from the dead as the firstborn in real history only recently (1 Thessalonians 1:9-10).

These elements of the biblical view are necessary parts of a worldview. Paul communicated all this and convinced his audience between three Sabbaths of teaching (Acts 17:1ff.). This was, to our best knowledge, the first time an apostle had touched European soil. This teaching, carried on by others through the centuries, laid the foundation for a changed face in Europe and gave dignity and moral responsibility to people as nothing else ever did. It presented a way of seeing reality that was coherent, intelligent, and historically accurate. It answered personal and philosophical questions and laid the foundation for a new, more human, and respectful culture. It spoke of the things of heaven and of earth, of spiritual food and physical restraints. It included teaching about sexual ethics, social responsibilities, and economic obligations (1 Thessalonians 4:1ff.). It taught an outlook on life that opposed death and demanded an alert discernment between what is good and evil, true and false, right and wrong, human and inhuman (1 Thessalonians 4:13—5:24).

The focus of this teaching was not an invitation to personal discoveries of what the gospel meant to the individual in his or her perceived needs. Paul laid out a coherent view of the world with factual and moral dimensions, with purpose and value, with a realistic assessment of good and evil and the mandate to be human. It was presented to real people who made their individual decisions about it, but it was never presented as a "personal" view. Paul related it to history, to absolutes, to all aspects of life, and to the raging philosophical debates and religious and political practices of the day.

In light of this and its results in the flow of history, it can only be called tragic that much, though by far not all, of the church has accepted a different view. A coherent worldview has been abandoned. It has been replaced by something more like a three-ring circus. I am tempted to call it the Barnum model. The edge of truth and reason, which had served us well as a tool over and against fear and ignorance, has been dulled by the effort to please and to attract people with what they think they need. The church has become a managed plant, an enterprise with gyms, shows, and dinners. Music in motion, choreographed movements, and emotional appeals are used to attract people into the inner circle of believers. The emotive massage replaces the intelligent message.

The motivation has more to do with the size of the fellowship than with the growth and depth of knowledge and practice in life. It is assumed that the size will indicate the weight. But in fact so much of this activity distracts from the rich content of what we need to know about the world we live in. A pound of feathers will not fall as quickly as a pound of iron, a lesson my older brother taught me when I was three.

The church has become one more attraction in the market. In the hope to attract interested parties, it has turned both its format and contents into something resembling more a circus than the church. The setting is now more like the Roman Coliseum with its programs to entertain the people and to distract them from the serious problems of life, which need answers. It is rarely the house of God where we expect to receive insights and instructions from the Creator on how to live, think, and worship. Barnum believed that you could successfully sell anything you have and do it in a way that people will want it, if you only market it correctly. It seems that many in the church have adopted that model without the integrity of telling people that it wants to be only a distraction, a circus.

Already the approach to this kind of a place is different, as you can see in many of our cities. You do not come across the wavy countryside on a road that heads straight for the church steeple, indicating there is a place where one can learn of God, of man, of true and eternal things. There is no tower visible as you come around the last turn over the crest of the hill. That tower in the past was orientation for the traveler in thought and trade. From there the safety of the town was announced. To it fled those who in the insecurity of the countryside needed a firm reference and protection and comfort. Its height symbolized access to the truth of the God in heaven.

Once again the Dutch painter van Gogh comes to mind, who, the son of a pastor, expressed the loss of content and his despair in the famous painting of the town nestled in the dark valley under night skies. The windows of the church building are dark. Its tower also no longer reaches into heaven, as it had done in traditional paintings. Cyprus trees, found on cemeteries and not in village squares, now make the connection for the artist between the world of man and the heaven of God, between time and eternity, between man's foolishness and God's salvation.

Much of the church in our generation has carried Van Gogh's lament further. Towns have spread, and the inner city has been largely abandoned in favor of cleaner, safer, and quieter suburbs or a spot closer to a highway. With this move sometimes only the members of a church know its location. What it teaches and how that affects the church members and possibly a wider public not even the neighborhood will know. The church is no longer a landmark in a place. It rarely is a light in the community. It makes little public impression; it is not a powerful presence to all and a provocation to some. The building may fit in with residential or commercial real estate. There it contributes to a balanced skyline. But its voice speaks only to the converted.

You will recognize such an area somewhere near you. A broad roadway guides the car past shopping centers, a gym, an animal clinic, and a carpet warehouse. Shops, offices, banks, and light industries are all in a parklike setting between palm trees, ponds, and parking lots. The names of nationally franchised stores and eateries are recognized and yet also produce a certain anonymity. They serve the town's human material reality with safe products in the same artificial settings. Safe, easy, and predictable experiences relay a comfort and nurture a fellowship of buyers where there is little community in space, thought, or values. Where in the past people would show off their clothes, their hair, and their homes, where children would run and play on the street or walk to school, now the year, brand, and shine of a late-model car is put on display.

In the same shopping mall and business or industrial park you also find a church. Nothing singles it out as a particular place, except when polite guides in their fine Sunday clothes direct you to a color-coded parking lot. Once you leave your car, you notice throngs of people moving from all directions, as if magically drawn to the center like bees drawn to honey or like nails pulled to the magnetic mountain in "Tales of 1001 Nights." The large structure, spread out rather than being high, with few windows if any at all, welcomes you through wide-open doors to the events inside. Carpeted hallways take you past many marked booths and doors to various rooms. Depending on your age, gender, orientation, or stage in life, you are directed to a group of similarly cataloged people. Others in the noisy and cheerful crowd gather around the booths or advance through wide doors into the main hall. It is one of those multipurpose spaces that could be an arena for boxing, a warehouse, a disco, or simply a dysfunctional factory or catalog store. The furniture is adjusted to the present purpose.

It is the place for four thousand members of a *fellowship*, the modern name often used for a church. The focus has perhaps turned from being the people of God to being neighbors or fellows to one another. *Church* always, by its definition, related to something with historic depth, a place of worship and listening, of reflection and prayer, a remembrance of God's existence and acts in history. *Church* defined a group of those called apart or singled out. A fellowship may still focus on these things, but often the name indicates a more horizontal interest than a vertical one. It stresses relationship with fellow believers rather than obedience to the Lord of the universe. Fellows are called together and gather. They *relate* to each other. They make up a group that comes to be serviced by one another. Few would come to render to God the service of acknowledgment, adoration, and worth-ship.

There is a powerful dynamic in such a gathering, especially since our modern life has split up families, neighborhoods, and genera-tions. Here a large number of people, the cheerful enthusiasm, the coordination, the event of a "happening" itself, concentrate every-thing and everyone on what is going on. Careful choreography, pre-cise timing, and multiple colorful visual images unite the fellowship into obviously common experiences, which are set out in a program. A well-managed team guides the audience through a sequence of exciting events. They sing, they weave and sway, they pray, and they share and give. Overhead projectors throw words of hymns and praise choruses onto a large screen. Close-ups of the members of the choir are also projected onto the screen. There they stand in loose for-mations, in small groups of different voices on the platform as if casu-ally united in music and experience. The orchestra plays, and the lights are dimmed. The continuous smile is contagious; the move-ments invite all kinds of fellowship.

Personal stories, anecdotes, and other illustrations from life, more funny than serious, introduce the worship experience. Even the study of the Bible readily falls into the format of after-dinner speeches, which start with light and attractive commentary. It assumes that people will more readily listen when they feel relaxed, amused, and on an equal folksy footing with the leader. This is a way of introducing religion to a generation that is increasingly unfamiliar with the old questions of life and death, of justice and God's purposes for us as human beings. Their interest is far more personal, immediate, and psychologically colored. They rarely even know that these questions are part of the human inquiry, history, and human obligation that set us apart from all other creatures, since the human being alone transcends his exis-tence and asks questions about purpose, about good and evil, about why and who.

Personal interest stories, self-help programs, recovery hints, and manuals for living now form the core of what used to be exposition and application from the study of a text. Times of moral ambivalence and democratic pluralism rarely create an interest in knowing how to live truthfully. Instead the constant focus and desire is to be sure that one receives the tools and guidance to experience life fully and personally. The intellectual and spiritual concern or interest found so much in the teaching of Jesus and the apostles is easily minimized. They taught, discussed, and demonstrated the existence and the power of God and the truthfulness of the law. That has been replaced by the sensual and personal interest of our modern age. Relevance to me in my situation is expected more than revelation of what is on the mind of God, the Creator of the whole thing, for each of us.

People attend this church because they like it. It is fun. I struggle in vain to find this liking as a criterion of a faithful church in the New Testament. The joy of the Lord must certainly be more than this.

What appears as increased interest in spiritual reality may be that only in part. The number of people attending churches and of participants in Bible studies across the country and the network of parachurch groups and mission projects do not necessarily indicate much about the content of the thinking, life, or priorities of people. It does not indicate how much is understood or sought out about what is true and right in the universe we inhabit. More often it may reveal personal needs and efforts, the longing for a higher dimension and for personal engagement in a culture that has been so successful in having scientific dominion over much of life.

Many visual artists struggled in the nineteenth century for a recognized place for their work when the newly available camera produced exact representations of the world around them. We also seek some form of personal affirmation in a world that we have materially mastered to a marvelous degree. We tend to express that in personal consumption of money and time, travel, people, and also religion and religious experiences. Here we find affirmation that we are not machines but are free and in a measure sovereign. More people may attend church, seek out fellowships, and take time off to orient their values and spiritual concerns. But when churches are selected along social, cultural, and aesthetic lines, they do not always meet standards of biblical discrimination. Whatever is found may please only because it is different from normal life with its pursuit of material gain and obedience to schedules, promotion plans, and career goals.

There is a deep dichotomy here, a dichotomy between what is confessed as belief and what is acted out in life. Absolutes of personal faith are more absolutes of a particular confessional perspective than certainties about reality. What is believed is more like an ideology, a picture in the mind, and a chosen set of values rather than a conclusion found after much reflection and observation in the context of an open mind, public debate, and compelling data. Such faith rarely influences personal choices, voting patterns, and cultural behavior. Other faiths in the community are observed only as alternative personal testimonies, experiences, and priorities. Christianity no longer challenges other views through argumentation or detailed reasoning, nor is there a willingness to review any faith in light of possible errors all around. The absolute is related to the individual, not to the shape of reality.

This dichotomy is evident in the little effect that the teaching of the Bible has on public life. Why does anyone hope that prayer in schools would change the moral climate of society when there is a widespread illiteracy about the Bible? The concept of truth has been democratized, personalized, and compartmentalized. It has lost its weight. When it is filtered through an idea of "personal truth," democratic relativism, and separated compartments of mind and soul, of private faith and public functions, prayer in school will only confuse everything more. Instead we should push for greater coherence, rationality, and evidence and seek to replace the fascination with ideology and silly religion in our schools.

Christ's prayer that the disciples would be sanctified by the truth—God's Word is truth (John 17:17)—is extremely difficult for us to understand in our time. The concept of truth in any objective sense has been abandoned. The proposition that reality is true in a certain objective sense or that Christianity is true to the real world of man and beast is received with a blank stare, if not even hostility. Personal opinion is instead the last resort, even by Christians. How you feel about yourself, your faith, your family, and God is of primary concern. Anything beyond that is asking for too much effort. And effort is put into careers and success, not into the discovery of what is true and reasonable. Those questions are far too intellectual!

In the past we could be accused of being difficult with our Jewish and Christian affirmation. No more, for many believers gladly maintain a dichotomy between believing and knowing, between themselves and the actual world out there, between their feelings about things and factual insights gleaned from science, history, and the word of the Creator. They prefer to cling to the unassailable subjective persuasion and call it faith and experience rather than have their propositions tested in the cauldron of reality, where it is exposed to possible falsification.

They forget that all knowledge in any field is based on believing the evidence after testing it repeatedly. Faith in religion does not do away with mystery, nor does science deal only with facts. We realize that all our access to reality is through limited perception. We believe on the basis of sufficient and good evidence, not because we have the insight of the absolute. The problem is not religious, but philosophical and existential. Our knowledge in any area, whether in science or religion, is always limited, unfinished, and subject to review. Tomorrow will add to, confirm, or contradict what we know and believe today.

The ready acceptance of a dichotomy by Jews and Christians is so painful. The language of truth is still there, but the substance has been thrown away. Without real truth, reality is turned into theater, and life into a show. There is an appearance of truth, but all links between words and substance, between what people believe and what they should know, are severed. This parallels changes in the way all of life is seen in the world around us. Once there was a common field of references, plowed, seeded, and harvested for the fruit of historic biblical Christianity. We are now in a world of individual farmers, each with his own interests, personal needs, and intellectual and religious relativism. Loyalty to an objective nature, creation, and history has been shoved aside by commitments to personal whim, fancy feelings, and private morals. Man made in the image of God has become the self-made man. There is still a feeling of absolutist certainty, but only about one's highly personal views. This, however, is more likely the result of an insistence on personal rights than on genuine conviction of an objective truth.

This shift in perception made many churches aware of a need to adjust their form and content. They follow the changing designations from "builders" to "boomers" to the "busters" found in Generation X and postmodernism, as we discussed earlier. But these familiar terms explain only initially different approaches of the church, while in the longer run a different content than Christianity is presented. The traditional, long-term affirmation of objective revealed truth has been replaced by an entrepreneurial focus on short-term projected goals. With each successive adjustment, earlier proclamation is replaced with current storytelling, exposition with sharing, and application with therapy. Forgetting a common humanity throughout history, with similar questions about life and death, the individual and the group, right and wrong, individuals are now visited in the beds of their own philosophical and emotional making. "Where they are at" is the more colloquial description.

Seeker churches assume they reach out to neighbors who they think still seek the truth about their lives, with intellectual questions of "Whence? What? Whither?" But by adjusting Christianity to people's changed expectations, seeker churches measure their success by an increase in numbers and budgets more than by the substance and content of their proclamation. They design programs that affirm the self-defined need of a generation no longer interested in traditional questions of life and death, justice and power, truth and deception, God and gods. When the message is adjusted as much as the method, the church meets other needs than what she is called to encourage and satisfy with the gospel.

Of course, it is difficult to awaken a person to a larger world when everyone has personalized truth and democratized opinions. A pluralistic society has made the search for truth more difficult. Much of our educational effort has created an intense self-interest in personal success and rights. The multitudes of choices in the market have created expectations that we can choose in any area according to our personal preference. This creates a mentality that God must serve me. The church service is then not seen as a service to God, a time of critical listening and gained insights or of expressing that God is worthy of adoration, obedience, and love. Instead it becomes a time in which a service is rendered to the visitor, to his needs and desires, to his tastes and preferences. Ministers of God become ministrants of the people. Dependency on God's Word is replaced by a selection of texts that meet my immediate needs and make the believer feel better.

Very subtly the massage of the ego has become the message, a distraction from the content offered by Christianity. For while we each have personal needs, most of them are defined from our own vantage point and bear the marks of our own dilemmas, possible perversions, certain selfishness, and a refusal to grow up in the real world. We like the fun and play experience of our search to last and to stretch out during extended, if not permanent, adolescence. Any message geared to appeal to people who are accustomed to shop around and to seek pleasurable experiences, to have choices in all encounters, will improve their self-image, it is believed; but it is also bound to be at best diluted, at worst perverted.

Most churches in Europe have little to say to our very central questions. A scientific theology has left Europeans with much myth and few reasons to believe anything. Kantian philosophy has robbed them of the certainty of knowledge by making it impossible to accept revelation in the Bible as the explanation of the real world of creation. Once the balance between the book of God's Word (the Bible) and the book of God's work (the created nature) is smashed, finite man can never know the truth in any but a personal and inner way. Kant is the father of postmodernism, that convenient invitation to be selfish, relativistic, and indifferent to the visions and problems of others and to feel sorry one can do nothing more.

Under the same influence the church failed to answer the question of human evil in a century that was marked by so much of it. Both church and society hoped for an improvement of man through education and scientific progress. The church hosted both hardened Calvinism ("History is the will of the sovereign God") and existentialism (announcing the absence or even the death of God). Both theological directions make room for every changing political interest, such as narrative or feminist or multicultural theologies. In reaction the search for spirituality is now directed in Europe beyond a silent and scientific universe to the East intellectually, to Zen and Yoga, to drugs and alternative mental states. Exotic deities have replaced the transcendent God.

Different reasons form the basis of a weakening intellectual and culturally effective content in American Christianity. Revelation is not denied, but the Word of God is much more personalized. The personal God of the Bible has been adjusted to the private needs of any believer. *Personal* is initially a wonderful concept used to describe the reality that we are persons in the image of God. He thinks, feels, and acts, and so do we. Being a person meant that we were not animals. We can act, while animals react on the basis of instinctual responses. Our relationship is individual and chosen. We love, obey, believe, and live not as a group but as individuals, not by instinctual templates but by choice and will.

But, as I suggested earlier, the term *personal* is now being used more often as a substitute for private and individualistic. A "personal relationship" is no longer the kind that is only possible between persons rather than animals or things. Instead it is a highly subjective relationship created by the individual. Affirming the role of the individual has brought many benefits to American historic and cultural history. In a broader experience, the practical usefulness of each person has been favored over the reflection of moral and intellectual criteria. The self either swam or sank. He or she had to develop survival skills and determine his or her place, faith, and life. It was more important to make things work than to know why or how they did.

In Christian circles this evolved into a greater interest in application than in understanding when it comes to the Bible. Pragmatism is a good thing in practical realms, but when it is applied to moral ones, something of compelling weight is lost. "What does it mean to me?" is the question much more often asked than what God wants to declare and explain to the whole human race, including me.

Personal experience alone is a poor criterion for understanding who God is, what he has said, and what plan he might have for my life. What worked in my case is by itself not necessarily true, just, or good.

This personal focus (how I feel, what it means to me, whether I like it) expresses a need to be the center of attention from God and men. Such attention is given to the buyer and seller in a commercial relationship when they meet on common ground. But when the same criteria govern man's relationship with reality or even with God, we make a fundamental mistake. For reality is not for sale. It is more like an unavoidable beast I need to know and work with. What I think of it is not a matter of appeal or appetite. Here, as well as with other people and with God, I need to have sharpened moral and intellectual discernment in order to know how to insist on what is right, good, and beautiful.

In all areas of law and life, of people with their problems, of religion and politics, I must consider more than just an advertised opportunity taken or rejected whimsically. The world is not a friendly place after the fall of Adam and Eve. The will of God is not obvious anymore in nature or society. This is made clear in the text, those letters from God after the eviction from Eden. The Word states the criteria with which all of life needs to be examined. Without them the appeals from merchants and media, from politicians and priests and prophets, even from relief organizations easily drown our critical analysis. We are left to like or dislike, to respond or to refuse. The church has a mandate to encourage more careful analysis, a more critical discernment, and more piercing questions in all its proclamation. Where she has not followed this, her methods to attract people have contributed more to confusion than to discernment. She has entertained the search for a better buy, emotional release, or just novel experiences.

Isaiah questioned why people consulted the dead on behalf of the living (Isaiah 8:19). By providing a three-ring circus at St. Barnum's Church, the living encourage the dead in their confusion, cynicism, and selfishness.

7

THE ISLAMIZATION OF CHRISTIANITY

Funerals in America are often elaborate events. There will rarely be
hired wailers anymore, as there were in past cultures. A different
set of rituals has replaced much of the reality of death, with its sharp
interference in the normal lives of relatives and neighbors. The
deceased are no longer kept in the family home until burial but are
whisked away, disinfected and embellished, and then exposed at a
reception in their honor in the parlor of the funeral home. This is
called a wake. As mentioned earlier, one advertisement suggested,
"You just die, we do the rest." Skillful morticians disguise the face of
death with their creams and lotions and a mouth filled with wire.
Landscaped cemeteries resemble rolling hills and parks, sometimes
with music piped in. Stones and monuments mark a place and time
against oblivion and point to the sky until the expected resurrection
from the brutality of death.

When death becomes a normal part of life rather than its revolt-
ing antithesis, a remarkable shift in the horizon of grief and hope has
taken place. Both are reduced, only privately held, not publicly admitted. Perhaps this is the result of our longer lives and exhausted attach-
ments. *As an adult, you have had your turn. Now move over and cede the
place to the younger ones in the cycles of life!* But in that case something
central to the biblical view of life and history has been made irrelevant.

Its comfort is reduced to improving personal feelings. Its message is spiritual in a perverted way. It no longer remembers the tragedy of life now and a future hope. Life and death are merely a part of the flow of things. The embellishment is an attempt to reduce the grief over the absence of a real and unique person. It is considered more spiritual to accept what has happened.

The message at a recent funeral of a distant relative is in many ways typical. A girl had died after struggling under her physical handicap for twelve years, supported by the intense, warm, and loving care of her parents. The pastor spoke about the plan of God for each life: God does not make mistakes. He had given that child to her parents to teach them these things, which they had learned. Now it was time to call her back to himself. In God's sovereignty he had permitted the handicap. Now he had decided on her death. This was good. We were all the richer for it: Lessons learned, sovereignty affirmed, events approved. End of sermon!

What an insult to the God of the Bible!

There was no word of grief, no admission that death stinks and is not part of the plan of God. It had all gone according to plan. Even the handicap of the child was a part of that, since "God does not make mistakes." The lessons learned by the parents had required the child to be burdened, to live a life of struggle and pain. The comfort comes from the belief in a plan of an inscrutable God who makes no mistakes and teaches us spiritual lessons.

There is an astonishing series of flaws in that reasoning that leads to sickening conclusions. The whole span of the Bible's teaching and example collapses as unnecessary. For if God makes no mistakes and if all that happens is the will of God, grief becomes merely a personal matter. It is then a form of resistance to the will of God. Grief is failing to see that everything is fine. To oppose death is an expression of doubt about the plan of God. Human history no longer takes place in a fallen world, but in God's plan. There is then no room for the word *tragedy* and no reason to argue with God about history.

Yet there is an even more serious question: What kind of a God would give a family a handicapped child to begin with for any length of time just to teach them something? What precisely was the lesson learned? Earlier Christians would learn to protest, to discover ways of healing, to improve life. But these parents learned to resign themselves to the plan of God. Happily they had not heeded that teaching in their attention and care for their child during those twelve years but had made every effort to improve the life of the child.

How much love, respect, and pity does God have for the child to make use of her, exposing her to the agony of her life, her struggles and frustrations, just to teach the parents something? And after years of building relationships, lessons learned, and effort expended, God takes the child away again so soon at the age of twelve? Or one might say so late—not before she had lived twelve long years! What comfort is it to know that you have learned your lessons? Should you perhaps have been a worse student, so God would have left you with the child longer? Wasn't it good that you did not learn quickly, for at least that way you had twelve years together?

The comfort of the Bible comes to us in two areas. First, we are told that death is brutal and the result of Adam's rebellion against God. It is therefore not a part of what God had made as a "good" creation. It is a terrible interruption of all effort, purpose, and creativity, but sadly real because of sin. Second, we are then told there will not always be death. It will only exist until it will be defeated as the last enemy of God in the resurrection at the return of the victorious Christ.

The Boulimie Theater in Lausanne, Switzerland, has had satirical pieces in its repertory. Its name reveals its intentions to throw reality into your face, much like a person with bulimia will give back what he or she has swallowed. Common occurrences and scenes from life furnish the actors with plenty of material to weave the cloth of their biting commentary. In the tradition of European court jesters they confront us, the modern sovereign of "the people," with scenes from life for closer reflection. Jesters were the only ones allowed to contradict the kings. In their humorous ways or in parables they pointed out contradictions, character flaws, and social evils. Nathan confronted

David in such a way in the Old Testament, because the king had slept with Bathsheba, the wife of Uriah the Hittite. Satire has been used through generations to laugh behind the back of the powerful. It is a way to question and to break through any imposed rule with all its power. Satire thrives under dictatorships and points out the failings of the system.

In a particular sketch years ago one lone man was on the stage in front of a totally black background. He faced the world, trying to make sense of it. His only props were a pile of newspaper clippings at his feet, as if left behind by previous occupants of this lonely place. He picked up one at a time and read them as if looking for explanations. They were death announcements and obituaries. Some just stated the fact of death with dates and times of the funeral. Others were introduced with bits of poetry or a saying of some Chinese or other sage. A number had a more religious, Christian statement, a verse from the Bible, or a thought expressing piety and frustration. They spoke of a valley of death, but also of fearing no evil. Others said things like "Her life was filled with work." One spoke of the autumn of life. The one that arrested the actor had a rather common phrase found in many religious obituaries with little variation. "It pleased the Lord to call home to himself," it went and perhaps it also said something like "in the Lord's perfect timing."

From then on we were woven into a web of comments and reflections from these obituaries. They drew us into and then spun us around in the recent historic context. Did it please the Lord to prolong Hitler's life? Why could he not call this evil man home to himself on an earlier day? Think of what murder, pain, and suffering could have been avoided if only God's timing had been a little less than "perfect." At the end of this, everyone in the audience was confronted with the pain and horror, the suffering and absurdity of life and death, of effort and evil, and the irrelevance in life of such religious thoughts.

Most of the funerals I have attended in churches say the same things, if not always in such strong terms. The sermons don't intend to communicate the actual message from the Bible. Instead they for the most part suggest that everything is fine since God has willed it so. They seek to draw for us some benefit, some spiritual lesson, some overarching purpose in the reality of suffering, injustice, and death. Reality itself is meant to be covered over with religious phrases to give the impression that what is wrong in our eyes is really right, in the same way that the Buddhist would say that what seems real to us is really an illusion!

In the dark world we inhabit as much as that actor, the hope of the Christian from his Bible has always been the defeat of death in the resurrection. The Christian and the Jew knew that death was an enemy, a result of sin to be removed as the last enemy through the work of God in the Messiah. But now, according to such newspaper clippings and many sermons, life requires our effort to justify an absurd situation. All of life is spent under the shadow of death. Every effort to resist death, to fight it with medicine, safety regulations, education, legal protection, technology, and moral repulsion, is temporary and therefore finally without resolution. Authors write their ideas to outlast their life span; artists make images in stone or on canvas more durable than their own physical presence. Parents have children to defy their own death. Yet in the end they concede defeat by death, which is at that point embellished, justified, and accepted. The only hope, that there would be a God in heaven to make things right, has been washed away in sayings that everything is fine already. There is no more enmity between life and death. The earlier Christian and Jewish resistance is contradicted by the admonition to a final resignation.

Modern Christianity has to a large extent moved away from the traditional teaching of the church about suffering and death, about good and evil in a relatively short period of history. This has and will inevitably affect the way we interact with and counteract a fallen creation. In its core the shift constitutes what I like to call the Islamization of Christianity. A particular understanding of God's relationship to creation, history, and the life of man formerly associated with the fringes has been moved much more into the center. What was believed by a few has become a quasi-litmus test of faith in general.

This view is promoted almost as a mark of spirituality. It covers over the real problem of evil by demanding acceptance as piety, while the Bible confronts evil with the power of judgment and redemption.

There has been an insidious shift in worldview from a biblical perspective to a more Islamic one, which consequently affects all of life, from work to enterprise, from responsibility to engagement, from moral will to social concern. The shift is a move from seeing God outside of creation but acting into it, to God being manifest in creation and driving all events of history.

The Protestant Reformation had reestablished a more responsible mandate for man from the Bible than much medieval Roman Catholicism had allowed. The authority of Scripture as God's Word to explain our life's context stood in contrast to the authoritarian positions of the Roman church in its historic weight and power. Europe always had the privilege and burden of historic roots. Athens and Rome imposed their marks on all of culture through literature and law, through art and architecture. The European is always much more caught in the inheritance from the past, molded by what went before. This expresses itself not only in pride of history but also in a sense of being caught, limited, and almost a victim of what went before. Under such a weight there has always been a tendency to accept the past as destiny, as the will of God, as inevitable in the run of history from Cain and Abel on. This remains from older pagan forms of fatalism, against which the Reformation brought real freedom of conscience, purpose, and identity in God's Word (the Bible) and his work of creation (Genesis) and re-creation (redemption).

In the exposure to a new continent (America), Reformation thinking was able to bear more fruit in moral/cultural areas. The past was known but did not present as much a burden as it did on the old continent. On new shores gospel freedom and accountability could be expressed more freely, more daringly, more creatively, and, one must admit, also often more foolishly. A new city on a (new) hill would shine more brightly and unburdened.

The Christian spirit could easily go farther in the new territory.

Entrepreneurship would blossom outside of the limitations of traditions, rank, and class structures. Personal ability would be rewarded, individual responsibility demanded. God's mandate that the creature in his image have dominion, love and work, and resist death could more easily be carried out there. The belief in solutions was unhindered by an awareness of limited possibilities and past failures.

Biblical teaching produced beneficial cultural, scientific, and social results because it brought together the creation mandate with the realization of a fallen world. Biblical Christianity continued the Jewish outlook. In America it was more independent of the constant reminder of historic limitations and encouraged daring, exploration, and experimentation. American efforts against evil, from the defeat of North African pirates to the abolition of slavery, from democratic efforts to the defeat of European diseases like fascism, Marxism, anti-Semitism, and colonialism, are tied to the Scripture and enterprising cultural mandates.

It is, therefore, very surprising to see a large number of churches now turn away from this intellectual foundation. When they accept a more closed view of God's sovereignty, they in fact embrace a view that would never have produced such benefits. A controlled view of history has never before set people free to do both evil and good. These moral categories are abolished when nothing can happen outside the control of scientific matter, as in the Soviet system, or outside the divine will, as in Islam, or outside the power of spirits and fates, as in African tribal religions.

Different results follow different ways of teaching what the Bible says about life. Our interpretation of the text eventually influences how we act in history. Human activities are informed and encouraged by words, ideas, and language rather than just by experience. An entrepreneurial spirit, a passion for justice, and attempts to interfere with natural events result from the creation mandate to make the earth subject and to have dominion over her. They are reinforced in the commands after the fall of Adam to work against evil, death, and a fallen nature, both of man and of creation.

This distinct biblical view needs to be seen over against two or three alternatives, which are extremes in any case.

First, *creative actions often become excessive when man pretends to be accountable only to himself and his experiences.* The selfishness of man is played out whenever he assumes a divine right for power. The only limit is what he cannot do. What he should not do is not his concern. Slavery, the eradication of Mongolian immigrants to America (known today as Native Americans), the breach of treaties, lawlessness, and the pursuits of industrial monopolies were consequences of an excessive and enormously destructive license. When the will of God is identified with "manifest destiny," it is merely a more active form of pagan fatalism, even when biblical texts are used to justify it. For the history of power is assumed to be the will of God, an inevitable destiny.

Second, *creative actions tend to be much more rare, even unthinkable, in a more passive culture in which people are informed about what is good and true only from inside their normal and traditional collective behavior.* When you are told and believe that everything is always the way it was meant to be, your response is submission or resignation. A flaw recognized, a pain experienced, an injustice noticed—all these things are then only upsetting because in your mind you are unwilling to see them as normal, rightful, and without a problem.

For that reason all the religions of the world, whether secular materialism or religious determinism as taught in Buddhism, Zen, Confucianism, Islam, or African animism, see the fundamental problem of man as being in his mind. He is called to change his thinking and become detached from his personal moral reactions to such events. Faith in these religions means acceptance of the status quo. All reality is normal, good, and necessary the way it is. The problem is with your way of thinking.

In Marxism you see yourself too much as an individual with questions, ideas, and demands for justice. Instead you must join the collective, which is being projected forward toward a perfected humanity in an inevitable progress of scientific materialism by the forces of history. Your destiny is woven into history, which in turn is directed by the material interaction of all reality, including the stars!

In East Asian religions you must seek to overcome your reactions to what you perceive as suffering. You train your mind to embrace all "being" as One, in which the difference between joy and sorrow, life and death, and youth and age disappear. You learn to be detached from such distinctions, to go with the flow, to float like a leaf on the river of time. Man enters the water and causes no ripple.

Islam is much closer to this way of thinking than to Judaism and Christianity, its belief in one God notwithstanding. For in Islam also everything is ultimately One. God is power everywhere and in everything. Belief is submission (the word *Islam* means that) to affirmations made, patterns followed, and experiences encountered in a collective around the world. There is no room for moral questions, doubt, or individual choices within Islam.

African animism sees all of life and nature as a hidden balance in which spirits and people determine all events. A person lives in repetition of what his ancestors did, for any deviation would upset the balanced applecart and bring trouble. There is no encouragement of individual life, choices, or significant changes to improve, vary, or invent an alternative. When the water runs over the dam, one will not raise the dam but will rather let the water flow freely and unused, for "it wants to live in Mombassa."

This necessarily brief characterization of religions shows a common threat to all of them. Religions tie or relate people to the greater, wider, longer aspect of "being" itself. The question of how man fits into the greater scheme of things is answered universally with teaching that man is part of it all. His problem is that he looks at it from the outside, from his own mind, instead of submitting to it.

When we recognize this, we are ready to appreciate the uniqueness of the God of the Bible and the difference of Christianity and Judaism from all other religions. Modern evangelical Christianity is at risk of abandoning this remarkable view. For it often straddles both fatalist paganism and East Asian spirituality. The God of the Bible is in his character now equaled to Greek fates or to Islam's Allah or to the materialist's energy: Everything is ultimately One. At the same time the believer rides a "personal relationship," "personal guidance," and "personal growth" vocabulary that makes his spiritual and intellectual focus the same as found among Buddhists in the East and Gnostics in the West. Thereby these fellow Christians embrace something of an oddity, for they believe two opposing views: Everything is in order under a sovereign deity, and everything depends for righteousness on their spiritual efforts of prayer, obedience, and sacrifice.

But that is not what the Bible teaches or what Jesus exhibited and lived or what the apostles taught in Corinth, Athens, or Rome. There is a God, and he created a real universe outside himself. While we are related in our material bodies to the rest of the material world, in our minds, souls, and persons we are first related to God in heaven. He made us as persons in his image, not in the image of nature. For in nature there is no personality. If we were surrounded only by nature and there were no God, we would be misfits in that nature. We would be alone and without an adequate explanation of the life of our mind, thoughts, and language.

The God of the Bible, God in heaven, speaks from outside human culture to give imaginative and daring ideas about what should be. The Bible does not just approve or sanctify what already is. Instead, starting with what already is, the Bible speaks of two possible expansions. The first is that of human creativity. Man was to have dominion. He, not God the Creator, would give names to the animals. Adam and Eve would have to shape their relationship, for God would not do that. It was theirs to create, out of two equal human beings, male and female. They were to have babies, make a living, speak, and design a life of their own making, for they were in the image of the Creator.

The second expansion starts after the fall of Adam and Eve, when with a certain playfulness they are faced with a broken and damaged reality beyond their imagination and creativity. In addition to what is, they now also have a moral obligation to struggle for what ought to be. This invitation to work toward what ought to be tells us what is to be done, chosen, and created. Of course, it also informs us about what is to be resisted, rejected, and destroyed in our normal historic culture. All of life is evaluated from what the Word of God says about that life. Without the Bible we would not know that anything is really wrong in the real world. We would only think there is something wrong and would be invited to change our thinking. But the Bible calls us to change the real world.

There is, however, a shift in theology and in practical belief confessed by many Christians in American churches, the result of two distinct changes in perception. The God of the Bible is first transcendent. That means he is not found in creation, which he had made outside of himself. (All of reality is present to God, but God is not present in all reality: You can continue to eat your sandwich, for God is not in it!) Creation is outside of God because he is eternal, and creation thus has a beginning. God made the universe distinct from himself, looked at it face to face in various stages, and saw it as good. He was pleased with what he had made. Into such a creation he acts through powerful intervention, miracles, additional creative acts, and his Word, both written and living. Prophets and apostles spoke and acted as God's Spirit directed them. Jesus came into the world and became flesh in order to bear our sin on the cross and to be raised again from the dead.

Transcendent does not mean that God is finished with his creation. There is no room for a deist view of things, which proposed that God once made the world but then left it to function according to its own laws and program. The God of the Bible is intimately involved with and personally active in creation, history, and the future of man at every moment. Yet the Creator is always the eternal, infinite, and personal God of the Bible. The creation is always limited, for it had a beginning and was made in the shape and with the definitions imagined and spoken into existence by God.

In this view the knowledge of God comes to us through language, his Word, from outside of what we see around us. We do not create the knowledge of God, but his Spirit informs us what is on God's mind. "Man does not live by bread alone" suggests that there is more to life than the stuff you find lying around and what nature produces. The more is "every word that comes from the mouth of the LORD" (Deuteronomy 8:3; Matthew 4:4). Concepts, meaning, moral directions, definitions, and explanations about purpose are not found in nature but in the mind of the Creator, who communicates them through language, grammar, and syntax.

This transcendent view has now, however, been replaced by a greater emphasis on God's immanence. By that is meant that God is seen no longer as acting into history from the perspective of his own moral character and will; instead God is somehow linked to the flow of history itself. God is found in nature, in the choices of man, and in the events around us. Nature now speaks to us and gives us clues about meaning, manners, and morals. What happens is seen as divine. The outside critique or reference of the *Word*, which allowed us to evaluate all events, has been replaced by an inside reference system of *events*. The transcendent God of the Bible has been supplanted by the immanent gods of powers, feelings, occurrences, and various life experiences in the flow of time.

We recognize such a view usually under the designation of pantheism. It assumes that God (*theos*) is in all (*pan*) things. There is a kind of animistic pantheism in African tribal religions. Roman, Greek, and Germanic views of the mysterious forces in nature as divine share this characteristic. In our own historic and cultural backyard this view replaced biblical teaching with the concept of manifest destiny, of God's own country, of the inner light, of personal convictions, faith, and directions. In his perception the individual person becomes the prophet of his personal gods. History is the divine script. Events are themselves the outworking of God's will.

An inside, subjective access to and interpretation of truth has then replaced the outside source of information about the why and how of life. The Word of God in the Bible is assumed to be the same as "my favorite text from the Bible" or a poem for that matter. By first making God immanent and then understanding what follows subjectively, the biblical notion of truth has been insidiously removed. First, personal interest filters both truth and meaning. Then the filter itself is taken to be the voice of God to each person "personally."

This is a tragic shift in many areas, as we have discussed before. First of all, it is not what the Bible teaches. The Word of God was not always personally liked, understood, or applied. Think of how often the prophets were reviled and rejected. The rich young ruler walked away from Christ without believing him. The apostles argued the Word, preached it, expounded it, and with it exhorted, encouraged, and clarified the views of their audiences. Any personal element of it was either on the side of God being a real person with ideas, feelings, and the power to act, or the Word was personal on the side of man in that we each have to respond to it as only a person can, because neither animals nor things have the capacity to do so. They are not persons but rather programmed creatures. Human persons have to read and comprehend it, distinguish it from other words, and then apply it by choice to their lives and work. The reason to do this is that it is true, not because it is liked.

The second harmful shift lies in the assumption that events, history, and life itself is a manifestation of the will of God. For then the moral distance between God and a fallen creation is abolished. The Bible clearly stated (and here again it is unique in all religions and worldviews) that we now live in an abnormal world. Sin has destroyed what God had in mind and what he had, successfully of course, made. There is a real moral and existential chasm between the original creation and what is the result of sin. Death among human beings, for instance, was not part of creation and will not always be a part of creation. God created us to live forever. The work of Christ, the Messiah, will make that possible again in the future. Sin, death, and the consequences of sin were not part of the plan or will of God. He warned against them before the Fall.

Death among people did not exist as a part of God's creation. He grieved over Adam and Eve after they turned against him and rebelled. They produced, by their choice to rebel, a new situation that affected all creation. They responded to the serpent's temptation and brought death into the perfect world, which God had finished creating at the end of the sixth day.

This understanding distinguishes the Christian and the Jew exclusively from the view held in every other attempt to explain life. Only the Bible frees all of us from the bondage to fate, to normal history as the will of God. All other religions outside of the Bible, whether spiritual or materialistic, teach that what is now was meant to be. Only the Bible shows a grieving God who fights a war to conquer what man has done with a perfect creation. Only in the Bible does God judge the situation now as in need of correction and then engages himself to redeem it. God never allows himself to be simply aligned with whatever happens. The Christian and the Jew always asked, in the middle of whatever circumstance, whether what was happening should happen or not. Related to God on the level of spirit, personality, and identity, we should always wonder and ask what the right thing to do is. There is no room for just going with the flow, the majority opinion, or the outworking of power in history. God's Word, not the events around us, inform us about righteousness, justice, and purpose.

The Bible portrays a God who runs after Adam to offer salvation, who promises his Son as judge and sacrifice. He declares that death is an enemy and not a normal occurrence, though it seems to be just that statistically. We are told to pray for God's will to be done on earth, as it is being done already in heaven, for it is not yet done on earth. Jesus wept over Jerusalem because they would not come to him as Messiah. He could not do miracles in Capernaum because people did not believe there that he was God.

The Bible describes a moral distance between God and history. God is sovereign in that he alone determines the outcome in victory and will accomplish it. He knows all things from the beginning but experiences them existentially from moment to moment. He is not surprised because of prior ignorance. But he passionately acts into a battlefield of sin and death to redeem and restore his creation. Often these are direct acts of God in the form of miracles and answered prayer and powerful interventions. But just as real and interfering is his Word in its effect on the mind of men. The Holy Spirit has given that Word and uses it to inform, to explain, to remind us of what is right and true in the midst of a history that is often very far from being just, right, and true.

The way toward expressing God's sovereign will is filled with battles and scars, which requires our moral discernment concerning what is good and evil, right and wrong. History is not a clear flow or stream of God's design and purpose. It is also the result of sin, rebellion, stupidity, and accusations powerfully carried out by Satan. The book of Job draws open the curtain for us to see something of this battle in the heavens.

Thus the Christian and the Jew never had to bow blindly to circumstances. For both of them, whatever happened in history was always to be checked again through the moral and defining lens of God's Word. They prayed for deliverance, for a change of kings and battle lines. They interceded against the sins of people, so that God's will would be done where it was not yet being done on earth.

This allowed the Christian and the Jew to contribute to the creation of history rather than just to submit to it as final or to tolerate it spiritually. The believer is the one who engages himself against nature's hostility, against the injustice of men, and against sickness and death in a broken world. There was never a reason for fatalism, resignation, or unquestioned submission in the teaching of the Bible or in the life of the church.

How tragic, if not perverse, it is then that fatalism, resignation, and spiritual submission to an assumed will of God, seen in the events and course of history, have become Christian virtues! What was characteristic of Islam, of African tribal religion, of the teaching about the inevitable march and cost of history in Marxism, or of the stars determining the experiences of your life and telling you about this in horoscopes has entered as a mind-set in much modern Christian teaching.

Perhaps it is from a desire to have no loose ends in life that such determinism has been made acceptable. The lack of freedom and creative responsibility is readily minimized for the benefits gained when we can be untroubled by unfinished, unresolved historic situations. We want to know that everything is in its right place. This is a way of avoiding uncertainty and chaos. It removes all tentativeness from life when we are able to look at events and call them good, justified, unavoidable, or necessary.

In the past people were in general fatalistic because they saw no way to change a situation. They were too small in their own eyes, too weak in their power to question or to change things. They inherited a long history of ideas and governmental or social structures, and with them often suffering and hardship. Their hope was focused on life after death. Platonic and Gnostic thinking, perhaps later even mixed with Islamic views of life after death, was always a temptation to the church from St. Paul's time on. Such fatalism, a willingness to have life be run by fate, is the common view in all religions outside of biblical Judaism and Christianity. It seems much stranger that now our Christian neighbors even in America, where there have been far fewer constraints from a long and painful history, have become fatalistic, even though their powers and tools to change things and their imagination of alternatives are so much more encouraging.

Perhaps we are more prepared to accept a closed and fatalistic position also from our habit of expecting clear and final explanations about how things operate in all areas. We expect solutions, explanations, and coherence. When we buy a modern convenience, we expect it to work without flaws. In the owner's manual there is an explanation for everything and a section on troubleshooting to remove every handicap. We think we deserve this in all areas of life. But acceptance or fatalism as an attitude is less the result of designing a better machine than of saying, "I will be satisfied with a simpler one if it only works and causes me no more sleepless nights."

Finally our culture, through careful scientific observation and experimentation, has been able to explain a multitude of problems as the first step toward a solution. This is so in the field of medicine, technology, and society. We could name vast linkages of conditions that produce anticipated results.

We have widened the areas of life in which we have adequate explanations. We can measure results from various conditions. Determinism seems to rule the day. Health and behavior, intelligence and the stages of development are all influenced and almost determined. Little wonder that it takes only a small step to assume that everything is already programmed and part of a larger flow. We bow easily to the proposition that finally everything in real life is like a machine. Christians see it as God's machine.

Yet according to the Bible and our experience, our choices are like a step into an open space. We assume that there will be ground under our feet, that we will be safe as we step forward. But the reality is that we cannot be sure. In real history we have not just interlocking pieces of a puzzle, but actors, persons, choice-makers who influence what will happen. Our security is that God has made a real and lawful world. He loves us and will redeem us. His promises are sure. But all this takes place in the context of a real history of choices, moral and immoral actions, obedience and disobedience, wisdom and foolishness. Our security lies in God, not in events of history, whether they be prosperity or death. History after the fall of Adam starts always in the seat of the accused, exposed to accusations and judgments from God and us. History continues around us, but it is not merely to be noticed uncritically. God is sovereign, but he is not the only player in history.

Many Christians link their version of sovereign determinism with the teaching of John Calvin, the sixteenth-century French reformer in Geneva, Switzerland. Calvinism is identified with the will of the sovereign God being expressed in whatever comes to pass in history. It is sometimes identified with a broader label of Reformed Theology. It is not limited to certain denominations but is seen as a mark of profound spiritual insight and an expression of faith everywhere.

If all things occurring were already the will of God, there would logically be no place for prayer, petitions, or intercession. The inconsistency between acceptance and prayer for intervention has nurtured a reaction in the Openness of God school of thought. Neither the extreme deterministic outlook of a portion of Reformed Theology nor Openness of God theology do justice, in my understanding, to the Bible. The expressed teaching and solid implications of the Bible give a different and far more ordered dynamic than is found in the order-liness of Calvinism in its extreme form or the dynamic of Openness theology. Calvinism in this form presents a God with power but with-out moral consideration; the Openness school honors a moral God who lacks power.

Calvin brought the biblical teaching to Geneva at the invitation of William Farel after centuries of Roman Catholic control of thought and life. Viewing the countryside from the towers of St. Pierre Cathedral, you can imagine Calvin's desire to announce to the popu-lation a different God and a different attitude to life than what they had had in the midst of constant insecurity about life and salvation. Low life expectancy, scientific ignorance about the plague and other dis-eases, and arbitrary courts and law in an insecure geography made life totally unpredictable.

The knowledge of God was mediated through a church that judged, like Job's friends, on the basis of events. People believed that God would solve such insecurity and eventually would heal, give eter-nal life, and administer justice in heaven. Yet it all depended on being able to deserve God's favor now, before one could count on God. What hope could the common man have when acceptance by God was a matter of an undefined quantity of merit, not a free gift from God in Christ? Forgiveness, justice, and peace with God were not here now but were held out as rewards on the basis of religious merits. One could constantly earn and then again lose salvation and God's favor. "If you did this, then perhaps; but then again, perhaps not, unless . . ." How much was enough? How long would it last? What if it was lost again?

Into this context Calvin preached from the Bible and comforted the people with words of assurance and grace. "God knows your sit-uation. He loves you. He has already chosen to offer you salvation by faith in Christ." God has elected to give his grace in the death of his

Son, just as he had given his Word, the Bible, by the Holy Spirit. St. Paul opens his letter to the church in Ephesus by pointing to such signs of God's favor, who in his very being is gracious. In Christ we have all spiritual blessings already in the heavenly realms (Ephesians 1:3). In the beloved Son of God we are chosen, adopted, redeemed, and confirmed. In faith we respond to the grace of God, freely given and not merited by works, "so that no one may boast" (Ephesians 2:9).

Calvin's teaching stressed the choice of God for us in Christ against the insecurity of the Roman Catholic view. Our comfort does not lie in God's program of selection, as one would choose this or that refrigerator and reject others. Election in the heart of God was not a choice to abandon his precious creation, but rather to establish a new creation through Christ's finished work on the cross. After the seventh day, the day of rest, the fall of Adam and Eve started an eighth day, on which God set out to accomplish an additional work of salvation in Christ. He ran after Adam and sent prophets and even his Son to accomplish the resurrection on the first day of the new week, the eighth day!

More recent Calvinism and much, though happily not all, Reformed Theology have hardened this into a system of selection, individual predestination, and determinism. The beginnings of this go back to a student of Calvin's, Theodore Beza, and the discussions at the Synod of Dordt in the early seventeenth century, about eighty years after Calvin's *Institutes*. In Dordt they changed the teaching of the Bible into something quite similar to the Koran in the view of God's sovereignty and his relation to history and creation. The texts they cited were taken out of context (e.g., Romans 8:23ff., Romans 9—11, Ephesians 1—2) in order to "prove" the total "control" of God, which makes all things "willed" by God.

If everything is finally willed by God, all opposition, critical rejection, or interference is out of place. Fatalism inevitably results, dressed up as spirituality. Material history is then made something both less and more than what the Bible describes. Work within it is of little importance. And yet history also unrolls as the expression of the will of God. Your spiritual and personal attitude about events in history then alone matters, just as it does in Eastern religions, Islam, and materialism.

Such a view makes Christianity no more different from Islam than if you were merely to add Jesus to Allah. The wonder of the Bible informing us that we do not always find the will of God in history but in his Word as a judgment in and information about history is thereby removed. The moral distance between God and what people and Satan do against God is abolished. There remains no more room for protest, no mandate to seek justice, and finally no prayer to change history. This turns out to be an insidious merger with Islam on the level of theology, coming to a common view of God. It is at best pathetic and culturally superficial. In any case it is an abandonment and destruction of the uniqueness of Christianity and the Bible.

Many Christians unthinkingly embrace a viewpoint antithetical to the Bible's view of God and man in the name of religion and theology. This can only affect dramatically the way we live, think, and order our lives morally. In many countries this has already contributed to an outright rejection of Christianity, for such a view of Christianity removed any grounds to oppose some of the more openly evil events in the twentieth century.

After the Roman dominance of all of life, the Reformation reestablished a very different view of life. It stressed individual responsibility to know God, to understand the text of the Word, to take responsibility for work in a wider world. It taught a relationship with God as persons. From him individuals should draw encouragement, hope, and love in good faith to work for peace and justice in the broadest sense. That view gave a gutsy courage to people, an inquisitive mind, an entrepreneurial attitude, and dignity to life and love and work. Yet somewhere that understanding has been perverted in two ways in many of our churches. First, there exists an unfounded supremacist attitude of being one with the will of God: "Let me share Jesus and my personal relationship with him with you!" Second, we have all heard in Christian circles one of these comments: "It was the right time for her to die." "God must have had something better in mind." "God in his grace took him home to himself. God allowed it to happen. He made it come to pass. God must have wanted it that way." These phrases all express a resignation in which again everything is the will of God already. Thus the petition in the Lord's prayer, "Your will be done on earth," is meaningless since, if this view is true, his will is already being done here in the same way it is being done in heaven!

These comments are typically heard in an Islamic context. Do we now also hear and read them in wide circles of the contemporary Christian church? They have a ring of familiarity about them. Both Muslims and many Christians state that everything is already right in their lives. Both supremacist and resignation statements remove all tragedy from history. Such words are used to comfort each other. But what comfort lies in hearing that everything is all right? These words invite the mourner to reject grief and the believer to reject judgment of what has happened. It invites him or her to become callous about some of the very things about which Jesus was agitated, if not even angry.

When Christians agree with these statements and find them a comfort, they have moved from a biblical perspective to an Islamic one. The change can be gradual and insidious, but they have redefined God for the sake of peace, a longing to make life in a fallen world less absurd existentially. They have found a way to make the experience of brokenness acceptable. It ties life up with a bow and turns it into a pleasure. They have found closure, when for the Christian and the believing Jew nothing is closed until the dead are raised again. They assume grief is a personal, not a moral cry: They assume it was accept-able to God. They have the doubtful pleasure of finding resolution or closure though the God of the Bible is still at work, "until he has put all his enemies under his feet. The last enemy . . . is death" (1 Corinthians 15:26). "O Sovereign Lord, holy and true, how long before you will judge and avenge our blood on those who dwell on the earth?" (Revelation 6:10).

Worse yet, such Christians have redefined God to meet our emotional needs. Our unwillingness to face evil head-on and to seek to do something about it has turned God into the one who willed the evil! In order to not have to face an unfinished, unresolved situation, an open wound, we turn God into one who is at peace with a broken world. Though good and evil still exist in the real world for real people, God now becomes the one who in some way authors and orchestrates good and evil. We declare our inability to understand, then turn around and suggest that he must have thought it to be good. We are no longer partners of a God who is at war with a fallen world, who grieves over death, and who has pity and compassion for people caught in a horrible situation after the Fall. That God has been banished.

We may not have noticed this subtle but radical change in the thinking of much of the church. It leads finally to immoral consequences. Where Islam considers doubts and questions to be blasphemy, it is equally blasphemous for Christians to stop the complaint about death in its many forms and to assume that God identifies with everything that happens. When we do that, we have in fact become friends of the friends of Job. Such persons overlook the fact that much on earth is not right. It is even absurd, disjointed, and full of contradictions. There is a war going on in heaven, with consequences in the life of Job and each believer. Life during war is a mess, and the just suffer without cause. How can we justify calling this the will of God or providence?

The will of the Lord is not yet being done on earth in the same way it is already being done in heaven. The Lord's Prayer encourages us to pray for a future time when there will be no such discontinuity. In the world today that disconnect is real and painful. There is no tidy world in the Bible. Tidiness was there at creation and shall be again after the resurrection but is not present now. We are not allowed to bow to fateful circumstances but are to question them and resist them, where that is morally demanded. Even Joseph did not resign himself to being sold to Egypt. Though God would turn to good what his brothers had meant for evil, Joseph rightly asked the steward to remember him before Pharaoh, lest he be left to rot in prison alone. The cause of the tragedy was not the will of the Lord.

The view that God wills all things on earth may often come from a genuine search for spirituality. We want to obey, to believe correctly, and to give God the glory. The trouble is that this is the wrong way to go about it. Obedience is not blind but informed. Faith consists of believing certain things about God and the world, informed by Scripture. The glory of God is identified with his holy character, a distinct, moral, and resolute personality who fights evil, death, and confusion.

Spirituality is not the opposite of thoughtfulness, but its companion. It is not an embrace of alternate categories and priorities. Spirituality is not irrational. It is also not an antithesis to material concerns. Spirituality in the Bible is the response with our spirit to what God's Spirit has told us in the Scriptures (1 Corinthians 2:6ff.) and confirms to us by his presence. When we are filled with the Spirit, we have more, not less discernment (Eph. 5:18). The Spirit of God will lead us into truth, not away from it. He will make us more sensitive to wrong as we read his Word and compare it with the reality of life. This includes wrong ideas about God. He will remind us of what he, the Spirit, has revealed through the prophets and apostles (2 Peter 1:19ff.).

Christ was grieved, deeply moved in spirit (John 11:33-35), and wept, troubled about such a hideous reality as death in his created world after the fall of Adam. To be spiritual, then, involves the courage to oppose the results of the Fall and to complain *to* God, not *against* him. You will show your submission to him in your refusal to accept as final, inevitable, and good the outworking of man's rebellion in reality. God's world is spoiled. History is not holy, normal, or approved. We are called to be holy because we are not so yet, being part of a fallen nature and history. God is at war against sin, and he will win.

There is no way to make peace with normality in a fallen world. The church has in the past championed truth through doctors, judges, teachers, soldiers, journalists, and others within her who dared to stand against the silence of nature and of the normal. They make no trouble except to those who want a quiet public in silent resignation. Justice is our concern, not peace at any price. For the only way to be at peace at present in our fallen history comes at the price of detachment, indifference, and ultimately in death, where you may, as inscriptions on gravestones attest, "rest in peace."

The temptation to find a way to approve whatever happens is great. None of us likes an unresolved situation. But life in the fallen world will remain unresolved until Christ returns. Only then will there be everlasting righteousness.

We must not make God the author of life in the real world after the Fall, as if he allowed and approved of all events in life. Foreordination speaks of both his intimate involvement in events and of the rational coherence of cause and effect in his creation. It does not include his moral approval of Satan's rebellion or the sin of Adam or the drunken driver down the road. He has ordained that punishment will follow evil, but not that evil will be chosen in his good creation. He is not distant but passionate. He not only observes—he acts. Yet other actors' choices also have ordained consequences that cannot be avoided. It is not as if even though God could have stopped something evil, he didn't and so is responsible in some way for the evil. We are also not to believe and affirm that something contrary to the being of God is still somehow right. Some see in all this a higher purpose, inaccessible to us, rooted in the inscrutable counsel of God's holy will, in which he has determined that a child should die and Hitler should live a little longer with his program of genocide. Some Christians end up believing something like this because they wish to have cosmic mystery like every other religion. But this is not the way to escape the moral accusation of worshiping an immoral God.

We cringe but are still told to accept it all in deep "humility." We don't understand, but we must see it "spiritually." We argue with it but are told that we are face to face with a "mystery"! We are told this is all part of the "sovereignty of God," as if that answers all questions of good and evil, judgment and righteousness, life against death. Yet there is nothing mysterious about the morality of God in the Bible.

The only mystery in the Bible concerns the Messiah, and he has now been revealed!

The Bible demands that we reject this submission to tragedy. There should be no insidious acceptance of Islamic thought by making resignation a virtue. This line of thinking identifies God with whatever comes to pass. Yet the God of the Bible is removed from what comes to pass in two ways.

First, God created a universe outside himself. He is not in it and does not identify with it. It was good before the Fall. Second, that good creation has been affected by the sin of man. It is no longer good but broken. It is no longer in all its parts the reflection of the character of God. Consequently we must ask God to what extent he agrees or does not agree with the way things are now. What should we do about life in a fallen world? What is God willing to invest anew? Does he approve of the ways of history? Where and how shall we oppose evil powers, fatalism, and death?

The Bible reveals a God who does not have other gods beside or behind himself. There is no one else to call the shots or to whom God needs to bow. He will accomplish fully what he has planned. He will do this in his own moral way. All details are known by him. He is intimately, personally, and directly involved in the whole process. He is not surprised by anything that happens. He knows the end from the beginning.

But, and this is an important "but," God's sovereignty in no way implies a total functional control. There are events that occur without God's hand being the only one at the tiller. For example, our prayer can effect a change. At no time is God's sovereignty limited by free moral agents, but his actions are affected. Prayer, like any action, changes things in history not only for us, but also for God.

Sovereignty also does not suggest that God can do all things at all times but chooses not to. Some things are impossible even for God *at this time*. His infinity is not a characteristic, but a measure of his personality and existence. His attributes are inexhaustible. His love or justice will never come to an end. But he cannot lie and still continue to be God. He is able to direct all things but will not be able to bring the resurrection until the return of Christ. His sovereignty does not imply that he could do all things by tonight. But he will be able to do all things *in time*, as he continues to work on our behalf, and his.

Some things he can do now, others later. He could raise Lazarus from the dead, but he could not give him a resurrection body yet. He cannot yet create a world in which five-year-olds never get run over by a truck. We wait for the return of the Lord. Until then we weep, but not as those who have no hope, because they do not have a sovereign God. We test all things and accept only what is good. We oppose evil with concrete measures, without thereby opposing God or defying his will.

Sovereignty is not a control mechanism. The Bible speaks of God being accountable only to himself. He is able to bring about what he has planned. He is victorious over sin and death. But the Bible does not leave a doubt about the agony, the effort in time, the grief of God in the midst of the battle to bring that about in the end. There is a prince of this world for a while. He has real choices, as do we. He is not yet bound, but he will be at the end.

We do God no honor when we deny the tragedy of human existence in this world. We are exposed to the results of sin from the past. We live in a world partially reshaped by Adam's choices. Why do we deny this, or at least belittle it by our approval? It is a false comfort to make God responsible for what happens, for then we deny that anything is really wrong. He is the real comfort as the one who will correct, not merely add to, the fallen world with the resurrection.

I suggest that the reason many like to identify God with what is happening in their lives is a fear of a loss of control. They make themselves believe in a closed sovereignty, for they do not like the unfinished situation found in a fallen world. Consequently while they advocate the control of God over the events in history, they abandon God to immorality. He becomes the author of whatever comes to pass. At least he allows what, in their eyes, he could prevent, if only he chose to. But since it happens, he must have decided not to want to help, even though he could have.

We abandon the basis for much personal and social effort in the fight against sickness, death, injustice, and fate when we submit to the idea of God's wanting every situation we experience. Job's friends held to that line of thinking. Perhaps the diminishing interference, the guilt about real grief, or the lack of passion in general in the face of any evil by many in the church in the course of normal but tragic events of human life shows that in their heart and mind they have become Muslims. When all events are the will of God, the only remaining effort is to make people believe that.

Perhaps that also explains why many in the church focus on personal faith and private spirituality, following some discipleship program for personal growth. The weighty issue of making a statement by our words and life for the existence of a God at war with a fallen world is easily neglected. When the proposed solution is to accept the status quo or to embrace normality, the focus will be on psychology and meeting personal needs rather than on serving the Lord.

Yet disciples will declare the existence and character of God, the Father of our Lord Jesus Christ, who came in the flesh to oppose evil, despair, false teaching, and death itself. The freedom of the children of God is not found in trained indifference to the reality of a broken world. It is rather the freedom to stand up and to enter the battle with spiritual armor, and to be found standing.

Christ did not model for us a way of accepting death. He came to fight for our life. In his death he won over guilt; in his resurrection he overpowered death. Healing comes when we recognize the difference and exhibit God's moral stand for life against death.

8

SPORTY CHURCHES

Interesting studies about the feminization of the church have been published in recent years.[8] They show how much the church's teaching has taken a turn to give increasing focus on the "softer" sides of life. Love, tolerance, forgiveness, grace, and an emphasis on sharing have become central and make up much of the teaching from the pulpit.

Sunday school materials likewise primarily teach believers to do things with a focus on developing social skills. We study Abraham to see how he worked together with Lot. We learn to trust each other in climbing and canoeing teams, so we can transfer our experiences to God if we are ever in a lions' den like Daniel was. We are told to love and accept. Life becomes more informed thanks to the experience of a campfire after a good meal and music. People should become Christians because Christians are having such a good time.

This is all perhaps part of the modern tendency to round out edges and to embrace variety in an open and democratic society. Inclusive thinking has come into the church to soften past and present exclusive practices. Personal concerns have taken priority over truth. Grace has replaced standards and quality expectations. In pursuit of personal freedom, we reject rules and responsibilities. Good works for self and the community, civic obligations, are easily replaced by favors and random acts of kindness without any sense of obligation.

But along that road we easily forget that we are not saved *by* works but are created by God in Christ Jesus *for* good works (Ephesians 2:10). We are exposed on all sides to democratic, progressive, and syncretistic ideas without steady definitions, patterns, and reasonable explanations. Our response to them is usually to pursue one of two extremes. We either get altogether out of the river of life, putting ourselves under man-made beliefs rather than under God's truth, or we just let ourselves drift, happy to be at least above the water.

The first extreme is embraced when all of life is made subject to rules and regulations. Those holding this view give the impression that we can always, in every situation, know how to be right and true. Indeed, God's realities are rooted in both Scripture and the shape of the real world. What a marriage is, how truth and honesty are defined, who God is and what it means to be human and to protect life, how to love my neighbor—these have precise forms and definitions that fit the real world God created. But many Christians go far beyond that into areas that God has not fixed once for all, where there is space for variety and experimentation.

Francis Schaeffer often reminded us that God's inspiration does not only touch the things said but also the deliberate silences of Scripture. There are many areas in which God has not laid down authoritative rules or directions. How many gatherings of Christians per week, who should teach your children what, whether you should celebrate Christmas, and whom you vote for or whom you should marry are not fixed in Scripture but are matters of wisdom and discernment.

The crowding of life with rules in all areas results from a lack of confidence in God, a desire to leave no part of life free from burdens of obedience. Yet many of the choices in life do not have a moral component. Each utopian, separatist, exclusive, and legalistic group assumes that life is an easy matter with obvious insights.

The second extreme is to make everything a matter of personal opinion, preference, and shifting priorities. In fact, reality does have a form and does not allow this extreme view with impunity. But the imagination can justify all kinds of things for the time being. That is the nature of sin; but it is in fact foolishness. Much of the talk about forgiveness, grace, acceptance, agreeing to disagree, and respecting the opinions of others in care groups or home study fellowships has little to do with either the Bible's specific teaching or with the world of daily lives.

This may be called the feminization of Christianity, but that certainly is not a compliment toward women. For both men and women, the real world has a form in many areas. God created a world of precise definitions. Water is not land, man is not a complicated animal, right is not wrong, and theft is not an acceptable method of distribution. Gossip is not truth, killing the unborn and the handicapped is not a way to give them a better life, and no one has two fathers.

Trust needs to be earned and discerned. But working together may also have to involve critique, encouragement, and firing someone for unacceptable work. I am not safe in a lions' den, for God has not promised believers that he will prevent all dangers or death. John the Baptist received the comfort that Christ was the Messiah but still lost his head as an after-dinner present to Herod's daughter. The biblical approach to life helps us learn how to discern, how to be alert, how to live in the light rather than in darkness, how to resist evil, and how to avoid pitfalls. We are not secure. In fact, either too many rules or having no rules creates an illusion of security and hinders the thought that I may possibly be fooled. Not all religions teach the same thing. Islam is not Christianity minus Jesus.

People believe all kind of things in and out of the church, without that making any difference to how reality really is constructed, how life functions and who people are. For centuries people believed the earth to be flat, but it never became that. My forgiving others without their repenting may make me feel better, but it also lets evil get away unrecognized and unpunished. Grace only exists where someone is paying the price, not where error is overlooked.

Reality has a toughness to it that is often overlooked in contemporary sermons. They rarely instruct about life anymore; instead they try to make you feel better, lay out a program toward that end, and then confirm you in your conclusions. They present your rights without touching on your obligations. They address your soul and leave out the material consequences of false ideas.

But anyone looking for wisdom, discernment, or realism in the rough-and-tumble of life in a dangerous world will not be satisfied. Is it not striking that people do not expect to be informed anymore by sermons that talk about work, art, and commerce, about wages, quality, and loyalty in business, about government and education, about life and death except where these areas are intersected by matters with a more personal focus—attitudes, feelings, and a sense of guilt.

It often seems that the only area in which even the church still speaks of rules, standards, and the real world is when it comes to, surprisingly, sports.

Mention sports, and everyone wakes up. Now there is a subject of a widely held, if not common interest with scores and strategies, heroes and successful business deals. Whoever knows Michigan mainly as part of the rust belt of the automobile industry or North Carolina for its textiles and the Z4 model from BMW is totally lost in that crowd. Europeans may watch a ball game on Sunday morning as an alternative to the concerts and other musical offerings Christians enjoy at church at the same time. Americans love to have it both ways. They go to church in astonishing numbers and still do not have to miss out much on sports. It crops up in a sermon introduction as an illustration for biblical teaching and takes up a large part of the conversation during the coffee hour after church.

A good game has its fascination. Teams and individual accomplishments, higher scores and faster speeds, close calls and last-minute goals make the heart beat faster. We show our admiration or our frustration over such things. Some people even bet on the outcome. Threatened strikes in American professional sports are averted when the President makes an appeal.

Nothing seems to pull people together as quickly as a game. Illustrations from sports in the midst of sermons make everyone suddenly pay attention. It is the next best thing to a personal-interest story. This is perhaps an indicator of the greater importance of sports over political, cultural, and economic references. I wonder about the deeper implications of this dominant interest in sports. I am troubled because the talk about sports so often substitutes for a debate over serious moral and political issues of our times. And worse, the patterns and language of sports are used to set the tone for public, moral/cultural, and economic life. Models, strategies, and goals from the arena of sports motivate a generation.

This is a touchy subject. Critique sports in any form, and you will be suspect to many people as much as if you had questioned their marriage. Criticism comes from all who practice a sport and those who participate from the couch or the bleachers. Any crowd of people, any gathering of even serious and successful individuals, will sooner or later focus their conversation on their one common subject—sports. Sports breaks the ice and is the music of socialization. Loyalty to a university is expressed first in terms of sports, not fields of knowledge, research, professors, and degrees. All other conversation comes to a halt when strategy, players, teamwork, and goals are discussed. To be ignorant of the best in baseball, football, or golf is to be ignorant of the center of the universe, the core of the world as experienced by neighbors.

Sports to many people is more than entertainment, a personal interest, or a business. It provides illustrations for speeches and sermons. It unites cocktail parties, boardrooms, and church session meetings. Highly qualified people, serious in their contribution to the educational, economic, intellectual, and political culture, today readily turn to sports as the real-life spectacle that holds the nation together and gives forceful expression to desires, a longing for success, and human achievement.

Italy and France (and I imagine also several South American countries) have newspapers wholly devoted to reporting on sports, and of course America has *Sports Illustrated* and other national magazines with the same exclusive focus. But I know of no country apart from the U.S. in which regular dailies, which primarily report the news from around the world and have only special sports sections, would decline in circulation because of a players' strike.

There must be something attractive and perhaps satisfying in sports that is not found in other communal activities. Religion, education, politics, and sex bring people together. But in each of these fields a measure of tolerance keeps us from applying more than personal rules, standards, and evaluations. In these areas one can make moral statements, but there are no obvious winners and losers. Approval and disapproval by us have few consequences in the real world when we are not in a game playing by fixed rules that, when broken, bring clear results in the form of punishment. In that context there are clear goals, and practice is rewarded.

When my son started to play soccer, I got to watch the young team members more closely. The game contains all the best of human social, educational, goal-oriented efforts. The virtues of self-discipline, responsibility, altruism, and dedication are taught, demanded, and practiced. Watching the game, the training sessions, and the crowds may explain this dominant interest in and almost the worship of sports in America. Sports, as taught there, are perhaps the only remaining area in which excellence is not merely spoken about but required. It is the only area in which rules are expected to be obeyed, independent of your cultural, ethnic, religious, and gender specificity. It is the only area in which accomplishment matters more than good intentions, effort, and self-esteem.

In training and in the ballpark no nonsense is tolerated. Ask a stupid question like "Can I have a drink of water?" and you are likely to be punished by a run around the field. Any distraction is similarly requited by a useful exercise. Argue with the coach or each other, and again you run. Nowhere else in today's world of relative values, multicultural ignorance, and progressive education is such discipline demanded and accepted. In no other area do people allow themselves to be exposed to such psychological pressure openly without resigning or walking off the field. Within its own framework, players bow to the demands of what is needed to play, to win.

I respect and admire the pleasure of sports, the necessity of developing your body together with your mind (*mens sana in corpore sano*). I am amazed at the control, the power, and the precision of the human body. I stand in awe before developing skill and acquired discipline. I am startled by the surprise of trained responses and creative strategic decisions.

In addition to these personal achievements, there are social benefits to sports. They unite a supporting community. They give expression to animated emotion. They demonstrate human achievement after strenuous exercise. They bring men and women, parents and children together around a common interest and provide a vivid experience of being one of a crowd.

But the absence of hardly any other broad focus for our contemporary society, with the exception perhaps of our response to 9/11, is deeply troublesome. Our society, independently of professions and social classes, is not known for its interest in the arts, its intelligent conversation, its search for wisdom, or its intellectual and cultural life. We don't expect to hear talk about history, the significance of a biblical worldview, or the cultural distinctives of Jewish life. We are not introduced to the wider world of the human quest for the good life in the various attempts and failures to civilize human existence. This has been largely abandoned in the community and left to the specialist with a professional interest. The fear of an alleged elitism has broken the resolve to insist on clear definitions and moral qualities. Maturity, as St. Paul suggests in 1 Corinthians 2:6ff. and 3:1ff. for the church, is also in our age no longer so important, when the pursuit of personal happiness has replaced the discipline required to pursue happiness through a moral and educated life. We tend to forget about the weight of responsibilities for ourselves, for the next generation, and for the things of God. Why have an oil change if the engine is running? If the wagon rolls, who cares about its quality?

We find a broader interest in the public at the time of the deliberations of the Founding Fathers. But we fail to see that the discussion about truth, reason, and purpose needs to be continued in each generation for the public interest. Without it we quickly lose the distinction between civilization and barbarism in our own minds and then in the larger public arena.

The wide interest in sports is no problem per se. But when this interest has become a substitute for the more markedly human interest in the world of ideas, of questions of truth and beauty and community, we have a problem on our hands, and it affects what lies at the heart of human existence. For sports certainly has not occupied that space anywhere in human history. We know nothing of the relationship between Plato or Jesus or Caesar or Beethoven or Milton or Goethe or Buddha or Mohammed and football or any other sport.

A few voices doubt the benefits of such a national fixation on sports. An interesting book reminds us that the promise of social and economic advance for black children does not lie in the belief in a basketball career. Most children who dream of dribbling for success never make it into the National Basketball Association. Those who do not recognize this fact in time never make it to success at all.

An article in the *New York Times Magazine* ("The Emasculation of Sports")[9] suggests that sports lost its innocence when mega-salaries began drawing the crowds and when athletes such as Mike Tyson, Tanya Harding, and O.J. Simpson became heroes. They were in fact spoiled fools and poor role models. Professional sports exist largely to hawk products.

I wonder whether the current and growing interest in sports is in fact a substitute to help us overlook the need for more serious considerations. Does the interest in the physical hide the confusion about the intellectual and spiritual content of life in a society? Does the interest in sports with a clear outcome after nine innings reveal a deep-seated sickness of heart and mind about the uncertainties of life? Does the need for victories by the home team and the accompanying military and crime gang vocabulary ("Sink the Navy. Trounce Wisconsin. Beat Oregon") to support it forget the need for a good losing team that accepts defeat graciously? Or is victory on the field or in the arena a substitute for the lack of confidence and moral certainties in other areas of our modern society?

Is the interest in sports an admission of failure to work with the components of a more verbal, artistic, intellectual, and moral society to influence the way people think and live? Is the interest in physical fitness and health a distraction from the failure to repeatedly renew the source of our culture, which lay in love, courage, and a sound mind with which to distinguish between moral and physical victories? Is it possible that the search for a good life of good people to form a good society, that quest and mark of Western civilization with its biblical and Greek roots, has been reduced to a game with rules and performers for mere entertainment?

Sports historians suggest that the values of sports have shaped, in some way or another, the American character. But is that character renewal itself being made impossible by the focus on sports not as a model for all of life but as the *only* reality with character? Since the game has rules and style, in the real life of work, family, and community we can be barbarians and neglect the underlying intention of sports, which was to instruct us in such virtues as playing by the rules, working together for common goals, and submitting to authority. What happens to society when even in sports the mandate to be a model is abandoned, and victory, not fair play, becomes overly important?

In addition, because it is only a game, sports has become another variety show, a kind of masculine and now also feminine soap opera. The story of such a show undermines the values a society needs to renew itself again and again in critical humility.

When the game is no longer the model for civilized life, it easily becomes an entertaining substitute for the battles in real life. We train for sports and put aside training for life. We accept the rigor of the games of Olympus but forget that the Greeks also gave us the tradition of doubt, of asking profound philosophic questions about eternal verities concerning human beings, civilization, and possibly God. With that selective decision to focus on physical skill and power alone, we have also replaced intellectual and spiritual discipline from the Bible with the arbitrary discipline of the rules of a game of sports.

My concern for the real things in life is grounded in the understanding that sports were only meant to entertain in life, not to substitute for it. The Latin word *disportare* means to entertain, to do something on the side, to amuse, to flirt, to divert. Sports were meant to give pleasure, to mock, to distract. The serious things of conversation were to revolve around the quest for the moral life, not goals and strategies.

In ancient Greece sports had a religious connotation as well as a military benefit. It was, of course, a training exercise for physical results. But it also expressed a visible reality of ideals. Human bodies, well-proportioned and controlled, exhibit a beauty not often found in the common things of life. The contemplation of the extraordinary, of greatness, would lead us to the awareness of a higher goal, a nobler aim. The power, virtue, and beauty of exercise would elevate the mind and stretch the imagination to always evaluate the personal present and find ways to improve it. Heroes were the people most unlike the common man and woman.

It was hoped and expected that the skill exhibited in sports would be a reminder of the challenge to develop mental and moral skills. As the winner had reached for more than what was natural to him or her in physical accomplishment, so each of us, as a spectator, is encouraged to ask the central questions of life that take us beyond the merely natural in us and the world around us. The visible conquest should encourage intellectual/spiritual discernment and mastery.

The Bible uses two illustrations from sports. In 1 Corinthians 9:24ff. St. Paul speaks of the need to run, to train well, and even to beat his body in order to win the prize of a crown that will last forever. To this end he had become all things to all men, in order that they might believe. In 2 Timothy 2:5 he speaks of competition for the victor's crown according to the rules as an illustration for the need to entrust the Word of God "to faithful men who will be able to teach others" (v. 2). Discipline in sports illustrates the need for greater discipline in the important things of truth and life. At the end of that epistle Paul was full of assurance that he had won the race, fought the good fight, kept the faith (4:7). Sports is only illustrative of the kind of effort to be spent in the quest for redeemed life before God in history.

During the Middle Ages, sports consisted largely of tournaments between members of the nobility. There were hunts for the aristocracy. Jousts were common, demonstrating the value of agility, reflexes, and training. Sports also could be found in the games between guilds to see who would catch a ball or some other object. Large teams would carry it to their village by clever tricks, smart actions, and agile bodies. Annual events like these brought people together and reflected on the community. They served as reminders to be on your toes in life, to discern between the good and the bad, between winners and losers. The game was an illustration of a deeper necessity of virtue, strength, and discernment in the real world of daily life.

Apart from that, games were often a substitute for violence, similar to war in times of peace. There were few rules until the nineteenth century. Games often turned into riots and were regarded as the resort of the idle, the frivolous, and ruffians who had no other form of entertainment in their otherwise harsh life experiences. Such riots with their resulting injuries, thefts, and other forms of cruelty could only be stopped when the "riot act" was read to the people, threatening punishment.

Church feasts brought the crowds together during town fairs and carnivals. In German the word *Kermess* reveals the link between church (*Kerk* and *Kirche*) and Mass (*Messe*). At such occasions, jousting and games would easily turn into rough play, with physical injuries and even deaths. Paul Johnson mentions that such games were called "camping" in Norfolk.[10] Later the Methodist churches would set up "camp meetings" to bring revival and to reform the "kicking [or] savage camps."

This helped introduce a moral theory of games—to lead to a development of healthy minds and bodies. It attempted to rescue the games from chaos. The Enclosure Act meant that games could now be

played only on a certain field by rules, rather than in the open countryside. Democratic ideals and economic development brought sports,
formerly a luxury of the hunting rich, into the reach of many more
people. An increase in benefits from technical advances and industrialization also gave rise to an increasing interest in health itself, as well
as the time to be concerned about it. In addition, the pleasures of rationality gave a mathematical dimension to most games. Rules, standards, and records established winners and heroes in a more objective
manner.

Here lie the roots of our modern interest, our fascination and our
leisure in sports. Yet several influences simultaneously gnawed away
at a certain innocence in what may have become at some time a wholesome and pleasant human pursuit. The new influences were restrained
as long as the intellectual foundation for life was solid and the components of sports were held in balance. Training of the physical body,
interplay between thought and action, concern for health, and honorable rewards for the winner and for a good loser (being a good sport
about losing the game) are healthy components of a civil life. Sports
within these and some other boundaries yield a sound social and cultural benefit. As intellectual and spiritual rigor can find expression in
physical work, physical skill can sharpen the awareness of the need
for spiritual and intellectual discernment.

However, the games lost that broader framework and were
affected by a number of philosophical directions and cultural developments. One distortion was the use of nationalism in Germany
against Napoleon's France in the teachings of Wilhelm Ludwig Jahn,
also known as Turnvater (or "gymnast") Jahn. His interest was not primarily sports as a physical exercise, but as a vehicle to carry forward
romantic nationalism. He sought to awaken more primitive forms of
life, closer to nature and more Germanic, as a statement against civilization, industrialization, cosmopolitanism, rationality, and also
against France. His student gymnasts and sports fanatics wore the
open tunics of forest folk with hunting knives in their belts, kept their
hair long, and wore the colors of and swore the songs of fraternities.

They embraced nature and emotions in their rejection of science and reason. They felt things deeply on a spiritual level; their orientation was more pagan and romantic than rational or Christian. They burned the Code Napoleon, the basis of all continental European law with roots in Roman law.

Their spirituality had a very sensual, physical, and nationalistic expression. It comes as no surprise that a century later, Hitler's National Socialists would continue the same ideas in youth movements, sports federations, and massive gatherings in sport stadiums of healthy and "natural" boys and girls, men and women for nationalistic affirmations. The sensuality, the group excitement, the use of sports for a drive toward victory, and the supremacy of German blood centered on the body, on healthy blood, and on support of "Lebensraum" for the Aryan race. Reason, education, and a trained critical mind were sacrificed to the political community of sports experiences.

The 1936 Olympic Games in Berlin were intended to be a demonstration of the supremacy of the German race. Health, physical training, and race science were all stressed from the beginning. The body came first; character and intellect followed only later. The Soviet bloc would later use drugs and training in the service of sport victories, which were presented as evidence for the supremacy of socialism.

A second factor we need to understand in the fascination with sports is the rise of visual stimulation and public pleasure in the nineteenth century. The spectacle of colorful and agitated entertainment in the newly discovered limelight and later under the beams of electric lighting would create a hunger for ever more. Unrestrained lust for greater, wilder things are a by-product of the greater freedoms and luxuries that industrialization gave to democratic society. The moral and intellectual quest was being replaced by a quest for more sensational things. Today the theme park similarly offers heightened sensation as a substitute for real life.

The theme park, precisely because it is not the daily reality, is a place where things go well and are amusing and always clean, while marriages, work, and life in the city pose too many problems. Theme parks, like sports, entertain those for whom personal effort is too frustrating or difficult. When the city or the marriage dies, a trip to Disneyland is hoped to give a healthy and visionary distraction.

The sports hero, who has achieved discipline and records, becomes today's exhibitionist. The winner of a record is admired simply for holding a record. He or she has become the Roman gladiator of modern times. Yet gladiators were honored in a Rome that entertained the crowds so often that its ability to defeat the invading tribes weakened. When reality became more powerful and crept up on the games, Rome fell.

A third factor is possibly the destructive influence of the democratic idea in our post-rational culture. Truth is no longer the result of revelation, facts, measures, and definitions that speak to the mind. Quality is no longer a rational consideration of what is good and beautiful. Instead, what is achieved, what can be sold and bought, is accepted as good per se by undiscerning neighbors in a world of self-made men and women. They believe they have God within them, and they feel good about themselves. In the past they accepted snake oil. In the present they honor easily anyone who can promise them something tangible and real, even if it is only an image.

St. Paul reminds the Christians in Ephesus (Ephesians 4:11-14) that they should be sensible about all of life. To those in Philippi (Philippians 4:5) he spoke of the obligation to "let your reasonableness be known to everyone." They should think about what is just, pure, lovely, and commendable (v. 8) not as a romantic escape, but as central to the knowledge of God and the foundations for a moral life. We should be sensible about all of life. This stands in contrast to the sensual emphasis of the pagans. In that regard we must acknowledge that our own cultures are becoming much more pagan, for we also make decisions very much on the sensual basis of what things and experiences feel like. Physical accomplishments count increasingly for more than intellectual and spiritual discernment. Pragmatic success is assumed to be the mark of a good life. Sensuality has replaced the quest of sensible understanding. We continue the line of reasoning we inherited from past generations, when the survivor in the West, the bare-knuckled fighter in New York, the fastest gun in the prairie— Jesse James and the Sundance Kid, for example—were admired as much as the good sheriff and the successful salesman. Here are tangible realities to satisfy the longing for certainties. By contrast, the emphasis on learning, on being familiar with human history and the history of critical thinking, was widely abandoned as an interest limited to the earlier American elite who had migrated from Europe. The new democracy was meant to open doors to the popular hero without regard to reasoned and revealed and then established moral categories.

There is a certain attraction to being able to reduce admiration to the physical realm, for the judgment is then not moral/personal but objective/mathematical. It can be quantified. This is especially so in a society that prides itself on its tolerance and multiculturalism. It frees us from the need to come to a verdict about the quality of an idea or an argument. The score, the numbers, the salaries, the fans alone count. What a person thinks and how he came to that position is then of much less importance than what he can do in physical strength, sales numbers, or ratings.

A shift to a democratic view of virtue involves the sacrifice of the notion of objective truth. Moral values are replaced by material accomplishments. In the world of sports, brawn matters more than brains. I must and do admire real accomplishments in sports. But that alone merely places athletes on a level with the strength of draft horses. Human accomplishments formerly were always a blend of moral, intellectual, and physical factors.

The fourth factor is perhaps the pursuit of physical health as an end in itself. It is dramatic to observe that this preoccupation coincides with a decline in the knowledge of history, the classics, and ethics. A dorm at New York University greets students with free condoms. Notices about health, safety, and meditation are more readily available than insights about courses, professors, and intellectual discoveries. An increasing nihilism in art, music, and the theater, in civil and intellectual discourse, is compensated by a search for the healthy body, heightened sexuality, and fitness as a kind of immortality.

David Wells, in *God in the Wasteland*,[11] cities Nancy Brewka Clark's proposal that for many, the contemporary interest in physical exercise is not simply a way of achieving or retaining health but is a kind of secular religion. As "churches empty, health clubs flourish; as traditional fervor wanes, attention to the body waxes. In other words, as the baby boomers approach middle age, a yearning towards perpetual youth flares up and denial of the biological takes the form of aerobics."[12] Wells suggests that the pain of a workout is a new form of penance; the monk's hair shirt has been replaced by the modern sweatshirt.

The quest for health and fitness is the one remaining area in which people can discover that they are significant, that they have control, that their choices do make a difference. For many, bulimia and anorexia are efforts to control the one area they still own—their own body. Having been robbed of any confidence or certainty in the realm of ideas and definitions, the only affirmation left is in the area of physical health, measured by chronometers, scales, and the use of prophylactics.

The death of God was declared by an abundance of religion, which then left the soul strangely dead as well. Only the body is still alive and receives all the attention. Our culture has largely rejected any standard in manners, grammar, and composition, even the definition of God or marriage. Multiculturalism has opened the door for cultural relativism. Postmodernism attempts to make certainty, truth, and rationality personal constructions and thereby obsolete. Large sections of Judaism and Christianity have watered down content and form by their approval of self-discovery. Personal testimonies substitute for theology.

Only the body can and needs to be given a standard shape. It is still significant and visible to others for their admiration and approval.

The biblical view of man and the world gave sports a place as a game with rules, played in the surplus of time and pleasure, which were themselves made possible when we respected a greater discipline and rationality in the quest for human life as instructed and defined in revelation. But with the abandonment of convincing structures in democratic and self-centered modernity, sports has become for many the sole arena with rules, heroes, satisfaction, and definite outcomes. Players are role models and receive millions. Executive leaders of states and businesses rally to their support. A players' strike becomes a national embarrassment and makes international news. This fascination with sports has become the only common discourse, cultural effort, and mark of real humanity. That is a far cry from a tradition that valued truth and ethics as concerning the heart and mind of a person, not only the body. Being a good person is no longer considered more important for the life of society than doing good things to one's body.

Not only has sports been emasculated, as the article in the *New York Times* suggests, but I believe that the fascination with sports reveals an emasculation of society itself. Precisely because it is only a game, it cannot fulfill its role at the center of so much admiration and such high expectations. As the center of most conversations, sports receives the same attention as the golden calf, an idolatrous fascination, and is the new model of character, in which the games don't stand for anything beyond themselves anymore.

To shore up the crumbling sense of self, people turn to sports. Here one can still experience the strenuous life and savor the precarious victories. For the sake of these experiences, fans overlook the change in the players, who have become a gladiatorial class. No longer models for ethics, they have been excused from restraints and propriety for the sake of our entertainment. Robert Lipsyte suggests in the *New York Times* that "sports are over because they no longer have any moral resonance. They are merely entertainment, the bread and circuses of a New Rome. Our current Babes are . . . some of the neediest, hungriest, most troubled and misguided young people in athletic history."

The growing fascination with health of the body and sports is perhaps more than a result of disappointed expectations. We still get sick and die. Immortality has not been achieved. Deeper than this, we are disappointed that our technological, economic, and material advances have not brought us satisfaction on the level of human existence, meaning, and answers to the questions always raised concerning the point of life. Like Rodin's *Thinker*, we sit in the Gates of Hell with our well-trained bodies and contemplate the meaning of it all. Too modern to return to the Bible, people crave the distractions found in paganism, nature religions, Gnostic secrets, and . . . sports.

We abandoned the source of morality, an ethic of life, that sports had exhibited and, by illustrations, taught. The manly virtues have lost their calling. Sports has become an expression of common life itself, in all its nastiness, its ugly triumphs, its commercial barter and success, holding cities at ransom and throwing commercials in your face. The loss of moral certainties that gave responsibility and value to rightful thinking, civilizing morals and hard work in community, has resulted in victory as an ultimate criterion—along with the resulting salaries, fame, and celebrity status. We lament the decline of culture, of education, of knowledge of the real world out there. We complain of unemployable youth and our declining competitiveness in the world. Yet we should blame ourselves for meeting our growing sense of nihilism largely with models from sports and body fitness. Our disinterest in the pursuit of the virtuous life reflects the loss of moral and intellectual certainties everywhere.

The wealth of a people is found in the moral and mental development of the individual, which will always include the search for physical strength. But in our search for success, we have bowed to the pagan attention to the body, to sensuality, and to pleasure and have forgotten the weightier concerns of a sound and sensitive mind and spirit. We have submitted to a multicultural relativism and have lost the definition of a moral culture in the process.

Sports and fitness fanatics may die healthier, but not any later, and certainly often less wise and virtuous. They have allowed a substitute to function as the divine. Their idol has lost its soul. This leaves us entertained but unable to converse about and to practice moral goodness.

CONCLUSION

A sign in front of a convenience store at a gas station in Michigan advertises "Liquor God Bless You Beer Lotto Milk 2.59." A Mississippi motel puts on its advertisement three lines: "God Bless America. Pray for our Troops. Under New Management." A church in Kentucky attracts people with an offer you may not be able to resist: "Free Trip to Heaven. All Expenses Paid. Details Inside." Another one somewhere across the country proposes "A Church Alive Is Worth The Drive."

The church is competing in the marketplace where God and nation, faith and sales are wound together in a bundle. Competing slogans and jingles that stick with a little humor try to make a dent in people's lives. "Here, me!" rings out as loudly as the "Hear me!" in the past, when the church was still thought to address all of life and to give an explanation for the why, what, and when questions that always remain at the end of the day in all of life.

Of course, there was then less to compete with, or was it more? Without modern access to multiple sources of information, without much time for entertainment and distractions, without developed notions of personal freedoms, the church was looked to as the source of much knowledge about God, man, and nature. She gave the intellectual and spiritual encouragement to tame any wilderness in man and beast across the full spectrum of life. The uncertainties of life such as sickness, death after a few years, weak laws, and undiagnosed diseases encouraged the search for certainties and explanations and hope. Now that we understand more and have securities built into our lives, the questions that God would answer have been relegated to the "also-rans," being seen as trivial and at best personal.

Christian faith has been reduced to a personal matter, a human-interest story, far less than what it claims to be and certainly was to believers in the past. We live perhaps at the tail end of a time in which the teaching of Christianity had changed indigenous cultures so they looked at life in a distinct way that honored human beings, addressed people's minds, and informed them about the world around them enough to encourage science, social conscience, and spiritual accountability. Where Christianity was taught, people were led individually to see the things of life differently—more factually and reasonably and as part of a bigger picture. We have no more indigenous people in Europe and few in America, for their culture was changed when wiser insights and more humane concerns came forth from God's Word and applied to all of life. There are no more Vandals, Saxons, and Franks, no more Goths or Lombards. The teaching of the Word of God emphasized our high calling as children of God rather than nature's crooks. God's Word and Jesus' person and life set people free from guilt, ignorance, and exposure to nature's fate.

The church, throughout its many ups and downs, brought a distinct content to the public. It taught but also protected the weak, established safe markets, sought medicines, and gave hospitality to strangers, the weak, and the unmarried. She started universities and hospitals and dared to stand up to kings and generals. She laid the solid foundation for the intellectual and social development of the Western world. The Bible's declaration of God and man, of law and liberty, is the only historic basis for all those secular declarations and pursuits that our generation values. Ideas of human rights, of progress, of caring for the environment, of equal justice for the weak and the strong, of review and repentance, of easing the pain of life through science and technology and compassion all derive from the biblical worldview. They have never been nurtured by another religion anywhere in the same coherent and consistent manner. People all over the world have sought them, but their own religions have always repressed them.

Only in the Bible do we find an intellectually whole and accessible source for man, meaning, and morals. Our world is unthinkable without the teaching of biblical Christianity in the past. By contrast much of current Christianity is far less concerned about truth, mankind, and rationality, about God and history, about judgment and individual accountability. Its focus is singularly on the personal self, and it nurses a more base desire in people to have their special way, their private life, their personal redemption. The Greeks, Japanese, and Mongols in the Altai mountains gave their gods the privacy of mountains in the clouds. We have gone further, for we have dethroned God and placed ourselves on our preferred mountain to be private there with Jesus.

This indeed illustrates a new age, far removed from objectively recognizable truth. It cannot surprise us that the believing Jewish community sees in Christianity one more variety of an old mystery religion: People feel saved and have private experiences in a personal relationship. Or that Islam finds our practice of subjective faith and piety blasphemous. For neither group sees in the contemporary Christian church anything that claims to be objective, true, and demanding a verdict.

The God of the Bible knows the heart of man but wishes to save the whole person. His redemption is made available for everyone, not for a few select who have "an experience." The Savior whom God speaks about in the Bible deals with people in their total being—mind, soul, and body. James (2:14-26) concurs with that when he says that there is no real faith unless it is expressed in works. Faith is not a substitute for knowledge, but the response to it.

The weakened influence of the church in our lives and society is partly due to bad choices people have made. Many read tabloids instead of newspapers, magazines instead of books. Quality has a hard time finding customers anywhere. We are constantly on a slide toward less effort, less coherence. There is something like a Second Law of Thermodynamics in all of us, which only constant effort from the conviction that we must create life and struggle against decline will counter.

But some of the waning influence of Christianity is also due to our not having the courage anymore to address problems biblically, truthfully, and compassionately. We prize feeling over facts, our own story over history (the word is derived from the Greek word for *inquiry*), easy faith over a more critical evaluation of firm certainties. In this way we emptied our mountain, Sinai, on which God gave the law to clarify what was so human in the valley and filled our hearts with rich imagination. Perhaps that is what Aaron also contemplated when he let the people make their golden calf and imagined that this was the God who had brought them out of Egypt.

We have succeeded in making up the loss of content with lively distractions. Man's need to know has been submerged under an avalanche of events, programs, and happenings. Reading the Bible for information just does not compare with a song-and-dance celebration. I still prefer a ballet group who work on their program to a church group who love it "unto the Lord." In fact we have mostly copied the attractions of the commercial world in a shallow and cheap manner. Why do we also entertain, form a club, draw people with sights, sounds, and short simple sermons? Is this a way to broaden our program, increase our budget, and start another building? Is this the better working magic, so we can measure growth in numbers rather than in depth for our roots? I once read something about "a sower [who] went out to sow. . . . Other seeds fell on rocky ground . . . and immediately they sprang up . . . but when the sun rose they were scorched . . . [and] withered away" (Matthew 13:3-6).

How far we have come from the determination of Irish monks to humanize the continent through their explanations of God! From pastors and priests who analyzed other religions for their inhuman paganism and stood against them. From churches that did not compete on the market of goods with their own products but whose teaching influenced both what was brought to and bought at market by now moral and thoughtful people.

The lack of intellectual depth and biblical, spiritual wisdom makes the church today so much unlike what the Word of God and the teaching of the apostles produced in times past. Who would still turn to Christianity with questions of meaning, purpose, morals, and law? We may have clear positions, but they are rarely reasoned out, presented with love, or lived out substantially.

The church has lost the wider audience because it gave up much of what it should know and in the past was good at: the light shed on human reality from the Word of God in love, encouragement, moral clarity, and compassion. This is partly due to the label we are too ready to attach to those who no longer show any interest. They are not so much the unregenerate as the unloved. They rarely enter the church not because they are sinners, but because they are shunned. And they in turn then shun the church when she has little more to give than watery lemonade in the context of a rather poor sound and light show. Such fare rarely informs and nourishes a needy person with a hunger and thirst for intelligible insight from the wisdom and certainties that God has made such an effort to communicate to human beings. When the church abandons her singular calling, she is usually not even very good in the attempt to compete with the street and market.

Pharisees in the crowd saw tax collectors as "sinners," but Jesus proclaimed to both groups the parables of the lost sheep, the lost coin, and the prodigal son (Luke 15). The good shepherd seeks the individual lost in despised employment under Roman rule as much as the individual sheep lost in the inhospitable landscape of life. The house is swept clean in search of the precious coin. The father calls for a celebration over the return of the son. Those are the acts of God on our behalf. But we must now respond shrewdly, as Luke 16 goes on to say, to set things right before the coming judgment. The former "sinners" must restore justice and truth. The Pharisaic elite and lawyers should expound and apply the Word of God they had kept hidden. The disciples, who still included Judas, must review their attitudes and trustworthiness. Each group then, and the church today, must stop the distracting practice of deceit and must dismantle the personal kingdoms of power and image.

"Christ loved the church and gave himself up for her, that he might sanctify her, having cleansed her by the washing of water with the word" (Ephesians 5:25-26). ". . . knowledge of the truth . . . accords with godliness"(Titus 1:1). Truth and holiness are more matters of substance than appearance. They relate to reality and the shape of things, not to entertaining shows and diluted lemonade in the market, which address our emotions and feelings. God's Word and history should lead to comprehension. Lemonade is valued for the lemons rather than the water. God will be valued, served, and enjoyed when our life and faith are based on knowledge and wisdom rather than on highly personal, faith-based fantasies. Religion, faith, ancient mysteries, and contemporary rituals may hold their ground or even rise against meaninglessness, materialism, and immorality; yet they fail to give sound intellectual and moral comprehension from the Bible about all of life.

There are no "truth in labeling" requirements on the religious market. Consequently we will have to be more careful and selective in our individual life and public commitments. Hunger and thirst for righteousness are lasting personal requirements for the kingdom of God. Yet, we assume to meet them too easily when our passing appetite for colorful and touchy-feely pleasures is satisfied with multiple programs in motion, growth figures, and the variable diet of affirmations, improved self-image, and participation in a group. The sensual has then won over against what makes sense, and the church revives only the attractions of a circus and the repetition of rituals familiar to us from the final days of a dying Rome.

NOTES

1. *Religious Congregations and Membership in the U.S.*, The Glenmary Research Center, 2000, gives one church, synagogue, or temple for every 1,049 Americans. Our figure is a rough estimate, since many ethnic and evangelical churches have been left out of the Center's calculations.

2. Marquis de Custine, *The Empire of the Czar, a Journey Through Eternal Russia*, foreword Daniel J. Boorstin, introduction George F. Kennan (New York: Anchor Books, Doubleday, 1989).

3. Alexis de Tocqueville, *Democracy in America*, Vol. 1 (New York: Schocken Books, 1961), p. 522.

4. Adam Gopnik, *Paris to the Moon* (New York: Random House, 2000), pp. 124-125.

5. See, among other places, the long discussion of how the "great obstacle [to discovery is] not ignorance, but the illusion of knowledge," in Daniel J. Boorstin, *The Discoverers* (New York: Vintage Books, 1985), p. 86ff. Further on he points out how the lack of knowledge (in geography, for instance, an orphan in the world of learning for a thousand years) was made up by a rich resource of ancient fantasies (p. 109). Often Christians would embroider a sacred world through doctrines and ignore the real one. This is no recent phenomenon, for in past generations Christians would often relish theological speculations and practice scientific and scholarly amnesia. They would approve pagan myths and Greek speculations but be contemptuous of pagan science (pp. 109-110).

6. David Gress, *From Plato to NATO* (New York: The Free Press, 1998).

7. Arthur G. Powell, Eleanor Farrar (contributor), David K. Cohen (contributor), *The Shopping Mall High School: Winners and Losers in the Educational Marketplace* (Boston: Houghton Mifflin Company, 1999).

8. Kaye Ashe, *The Feminization of the Church* (Lanham, MD: Sheed & Ward, 1998). See also Leon J. Podles, *The Church Impotent: The Feminization of Christianity* (Dallas: Spence Publishing, 1999).

9. "The Emasculation of Sports," *New York Times Magazine*, April 2, 1995.

10. Paul Johnson, *The Birth of the Modern, 1815-1830* (New York: Harper, 1999), p. 704ff.

11. David Wells, *God in the Wasteland* (Grand Rapids, MI: Eerdmans, 1994), p. 52.

12. "Faith in the Flesh: An Essay on Secular Society's Preoccupation with Life [Somewhat] Eternal," *Lynn Magazine*, October 1985, p. 18.

INDEX

French Revolution, the, 13
Freud, Sigmund, 27
From Plato to NATO (Gress), 99

Galileo, 78
Generation X, 146
Germany, 11, 21, 33, 34, 35, 36, 42, 43, 93, 136, 162, 190, 191
Gladiators, the, 192
Gnostics, 160, 166, 196
God in the Wasteland (Wells), 53, 194
Golden calf, the, 120, 195, 200
Gopnik, Adam, 21
Gospel of Christian Atheism, the, 133
Grace of God, the, 30, 73, 74, 85, 86, 127, 128, 168, 169, 179, 181
Greece, the Greeks, 11, 13, 23, 30, 42, 83, 98, 111, 134, 136, 137, 156, 160, 162, 187, 188, 199
Green movement, the, 36
Gress, David, 99
Grief, 151, 152, 171, 173, 176, 177
Guilt, 33, 83, 89, 128, 130, 138, 177, 182

Habakkuk, 37
Happiness, 56, 125, 185
  pursuit of, 24
Harding, Tanya, 186
Healey, Jane, 115
Health issues, clubs, 11, 194
Heresy, 101
Herod's daughter, 181
"Higher criticism," 30
Hinduism, 87, 103
History, 10, 11, 12, 23, 24, 26, 30, 37, 42, 47, 52, 56, 57, 58, 59, 60, 74, 79, 85, 89, 90, 101, 123, 124, 130, 133, 136, 137, 138, 141, 146, 148, 151, 152, 155, 156, 157, 158, 159, 162, 163, 164, 165, 166, 167, 169, 170, 171, 173, 174, 175, 176, 185, 186, 193, 199, 200, 202
  church, 11, 37
  cyclical view of, 99, 137
  fatalistic view of, 99
  linear, 11, 83, 99, 137
  prophetic history, 79
Hitler, Adolf, 29, 31, 42, 62, 63, 102, 154, 191
Hofer, Eric, 86
Holland, 17
Holy Alliance, the, 13

Humanism, 29, 34
  a healthy, 26
Human rights, 198

Idealism, 13, 23, 41
Image of God, human beings made in, 29, 51, 60, 89, 90, 95, 105, 130, 136, 146, 148, 160
"Inalienable rights," 37
India, 41
Individualism, 28
Individual rights, 9, 10, 11, 24, 37, 55, 59, 131, 132, 146, 147, 158, 159 see also *"Inalienable rights"*
Inner light, 40, 53, 60, 91, 162
Institutes (Calvin), 169
Irrationality, 24, 26, 30, 35, 36, 46, 136, 173
Isaac, 80
Isaiah, 150
Islam, 11, 36, 78, 87, 98, 126, 136, 157, 158, 159, 160, 165, 166, 170, 171, 172, 175, 177, 181, 199
Italy, 17, 33, 34, 183

Jahn, Wilhelm Ludwig, 190
  Turnvater Jahn, 190
James, Jesse, 193
Japan, 43, 199
Jehovah's Witnesses, 103
Jeremiah, 37
Jesters, court, 153
Job, 37, 58, 168, 172, 177
Johnson, Paul, 189
John the Baptist, 181
Joseph, the patriarch, 172
Joshua, 76
Judaism, Jewish community, thought, and life, 10, 11, 12, 30, 31, 41, 51, 52, 92, 98, 100, 129, 136, 145, 155, 157, 159, 164, 165, 166, 171, 185, 194, 199
Judas, 201
Judgment, 11, 37, 83, 124, 138, 156, 170, 171, 199, 201
Justice, 38, 41, 57, 77, 97, 132, 146, 157, 158, 164, 168, 170, 174, 175, 198

Kaminer, Wendy, 92
Kantian thought, 27, 147
Kenya, 42
Kierkegaard, Søren, 22, 35
Lausanne, Switzerland, 97, 153
Lazarus, 176